NOT YOUR USUAL Workbook

cat - c + b = bat

2 + 3 = 3 + 2

K

SUPPORTS • SUPPORTS • SUPPORTS
Current
State
Standards
SUPPORTS • SUPPORTS

Thinking Kids®
Carson-Dellosa Publishing LLC
Greensboro, North Carolina

Thinking Kids®
Carson-Dellosa Publishing LLC
P.O. Box 35665
Greensboro, NC 27425 USA

© 2017 Carson-Dellosa Publishing LLC. Except as permitted under the United States Copyright Act, no part of this publication may be reproduced, stored, or distributed in any form or by any means (mechanically, electronically, recording, etc.) without the prior written consent of Carson-Dellosa Publishing LLC. Thinking Kids® is an imprint of Carson-Dellosa Publishing LLC.

Printed in the USA • All rights reserved.
01-335157784

ISBN 978-1-4838-3491-7

Contents

Awesome Activities for Practicing Math Skills

Awesome Activities for Practicing Language Arts Skills

Count the bears. Then, connect the dots in order to show how many. Color the number.

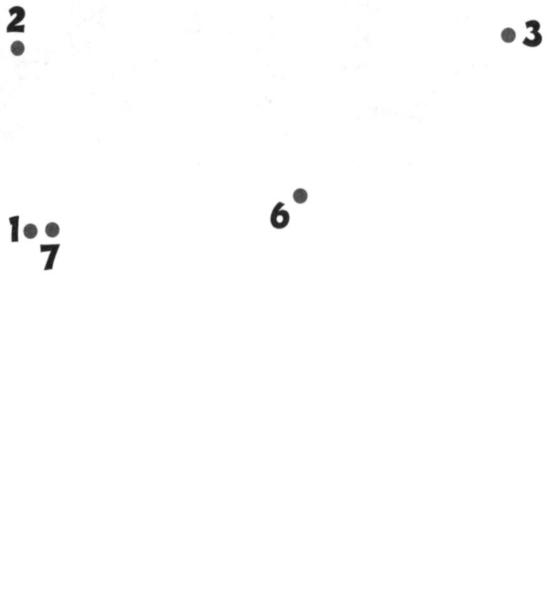

ON THE DOT

Skill: Counting

2

•3

1••
7

6•

5•

•4

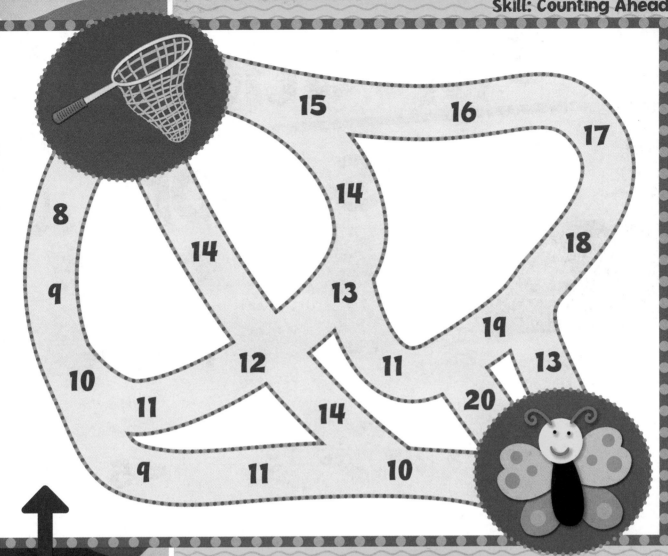

15 16 17

14

8 14 18

9 13

12 19 13

11 10 11 20

10

11 14

9 11 10

Catch the butterfly! Draw a path from 8 to 20.

Math ↑path↑

e(quation)
sen+sation

Write the missing numbers.

$$2 + \boxed{} = 5$$

$$\boxed{} + 5 = 9$$

$$\boxed{} + 4 = 8$$

A Show of Hands

Least

Most

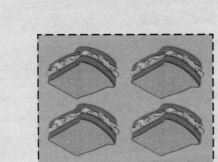

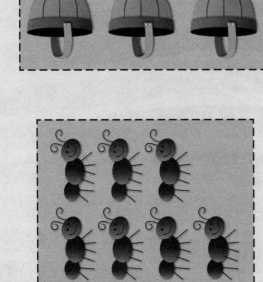

Cut out the groups. Then, tape or glue them on the page in order from most to least.

Skill: Comparing groups

On the Lookout!

How many?

Skills:
Counting, Recognizing Numbers

Write the number that tells how many bees you count. Then, color that number each time you see it in the puzzle. Look at the boxes you colored. What letter do you see?

Draw a big square. Decorate the inside of it with circles. Color your drawing.

DRAW

Skill: Drawing Shapes

STORY STUMPERS

Skill: Word Problems

Solve each story problem. Draw Xs on the pictures to help you find the answers.

1. There are 5 birds in the tree. Then, 2 birds fly away. How many birds are left in the tree?

⬚ birds

2. There are 6 turtles on a log. Then, 1 turtle swims away. How many turtles are left on the log?

⬚ turtles

3. There are 8 rabbits in the yard. Then, 4 rabbits hop away. How many rabbits are left in the yard?

⬚ rabbits

NUMBER CROSS

Count forward across each row and down each column. Write the missing numbers.

		3		
	5			6
6		7		
9			10	

2 4

3 11 7 9 8 6 10 4 5

PATTERN POWER

9 [ ] 5 3 [ ]

8 7 [ ] 5 [ ]

10 [ ] [ ] 4 2

12 9 [ ] [ ] 0

**Find the subtraction pattern in each row.
Write the missing numbers.**

SHAPE MASTER

Color the squares red.
Color the circles green.
Color the triangles orange.

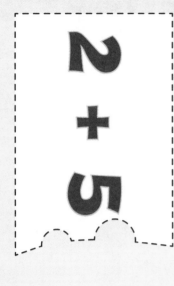

2 + 5

5 + 3

3 + 6

= 8

= 9

= 7

1 + 5

= 6

IT FITS!

Cut out the pieces. Fit each addition problem with its sum.

GUESS AGAIN

Read the clues.
Write each secret number.

It is more than 5.

It is less than 7.

It is the number of eggs in half a dozen.

Secret Number:

It is more than 3.

It is less than 5.

It is the number of your hands and feet together.

Secret Number:

Skill: Counting

It is more than 8.

It is less than 10.

It is the number of wheels on 3 tricycles.

Secret Number:

It is more than 7.

It is less than 9.

It is the number of arms on an octopus.

Secret Number:

Magic Square

Add the numbers shown by the playing cards in each row and column. Write the sums in the boxes. Ace cards equal one.

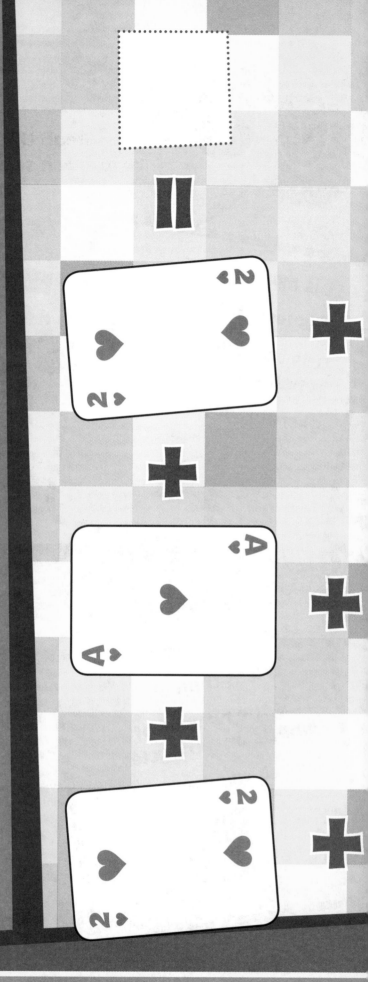

DARE TO DECODE

Skill: Subtraction

Use the code to find the numbers. Then, solve the problems.

Code Key

🍉	🍪	🥪	🍽️	🍎
2	4	5	7	8

□ - □ = □

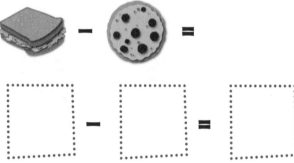

□ - □ = □

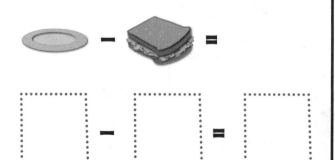

□ - □ = □

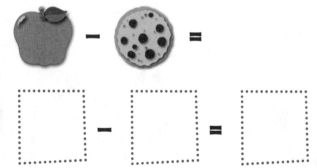

□ - □ = □

Each row shows a group of 10 plus some more. Write how many in all.

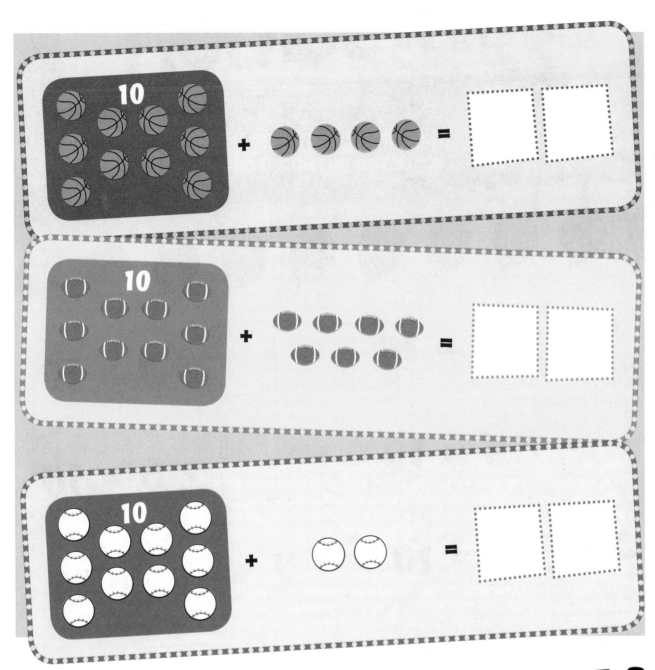

Picture Perfect!

e(quation)
sen+sation

How many more are needed to make 10?
Write the missing numbers.

$5 + \boxed{} = 10$

$\boxed{} + 1 = 10$

$\boxed{} + 4 = 10$

$\boxed{} + 6 = 10$

$3 + \boxed{} = 10$

$7 + \boxed{} = 10$

$\boxed{} + 8 = 10$

$10 + \boxed{} = 10$

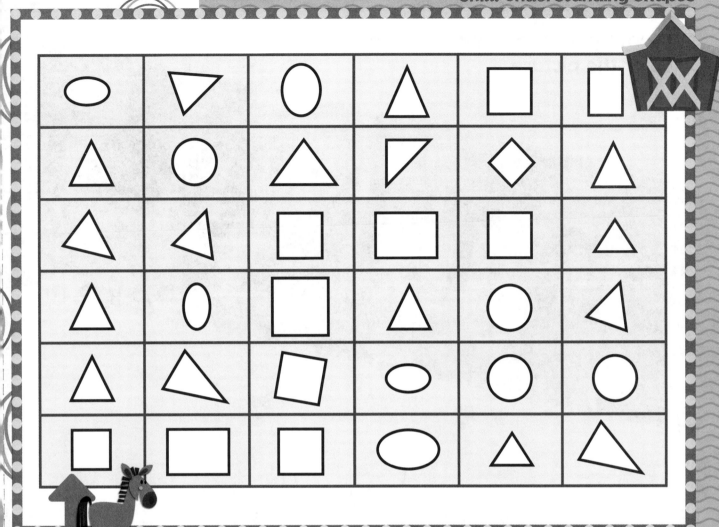

Help the horse get back to the barn. Make a path by coloring the shapes that have four sides.

Math ↑path↓

**Count by tens to connect the dots.
Color the picture.**

Skill: Counting by Tens

A Show of Hands

Skills: Counting, Classifying

Cut out each picture. Does it show an animal that lives in water or an animal that lives on land? Glue or tape each picture where it belongs. Write a number to tell how many are in each group.

Water Animals

How many?

Land Animals

How many?

On the Lookout!

15	13	20	17	19
14	12	19	16	18
13	11	18	15	17
12	10	17	14	16

10 ones and 4 ones

10 ones and 2 ones

10 ones and 7 ones

10 ones and 5 ones

10 ones and 9 ones

Skill: Place Value

Read each description. Circle the correct number.

STORY STUMPERS

Skill: Word Problems

Solve each story problem. Use the pictures to help you find the answer.

1. There were 5 trees in the yard. We planted 3 more trees. How many trees are in the yard now?

☐ trees

2. 4 frogs croaked. Then, 3 more frogs began to croak. How many frogs were croaking in all?

☐ frogs

3. 6 cars were parked in a lot. Then, 2 more cars parked there. How many cars in all were parked in the lot?

☐ cars

Use the four small triangles to draw one big triangle. Use the four small squares to draw one big square.

DRAW

Skill: Drawing Shapes

QUICK

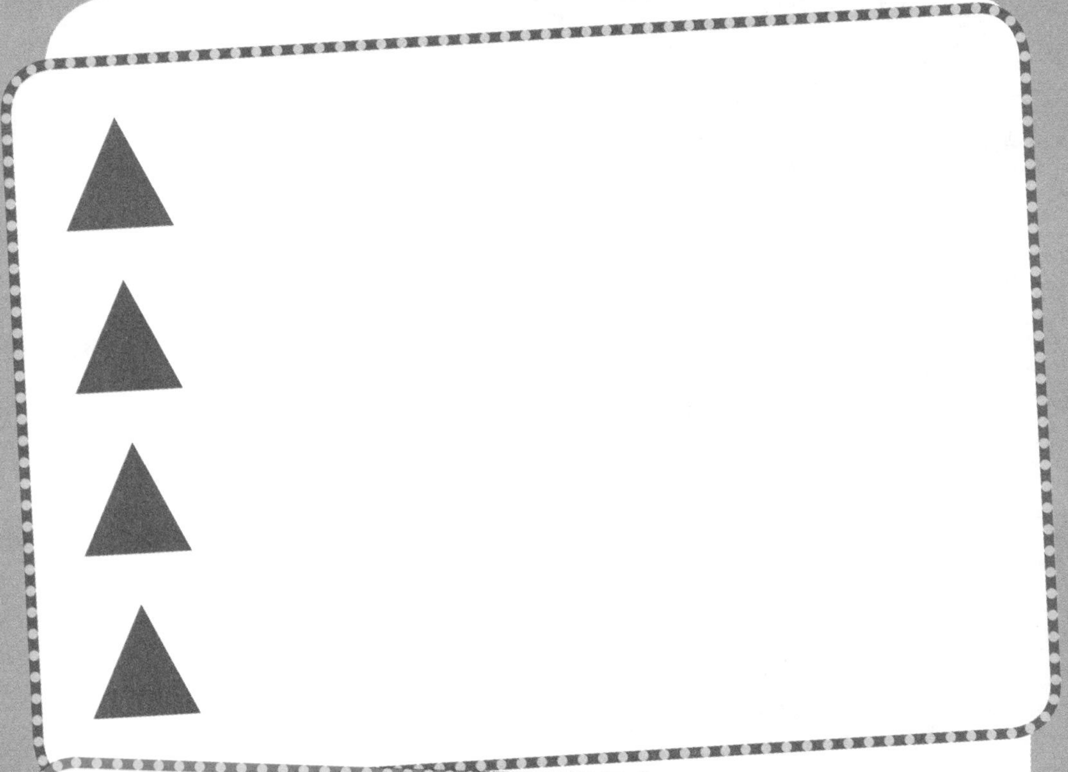

NUMBER CROSS

1. $2 + 7 =$ _____

2. $2 + 6 =$ _____

3. $2 + 5 =$ _____

4. $2 + 4 =$ _____

5. $2 + 3 =$ _____

6. $9 - 5 =$ _____

7. $9 - 6 =$ _____

8. $9 - 7 =$ _____

9. $9 - 8 =$ _____

Solve each problem. Write the answer in the puzzle.

SHAPE MASTER

How many triangles can you find in the drawing? Write the number.

Triangles:

Magic Square

The sum of the numbers in each row is 8. The sum of the numbers in each column is 8. Write the missing numbers.

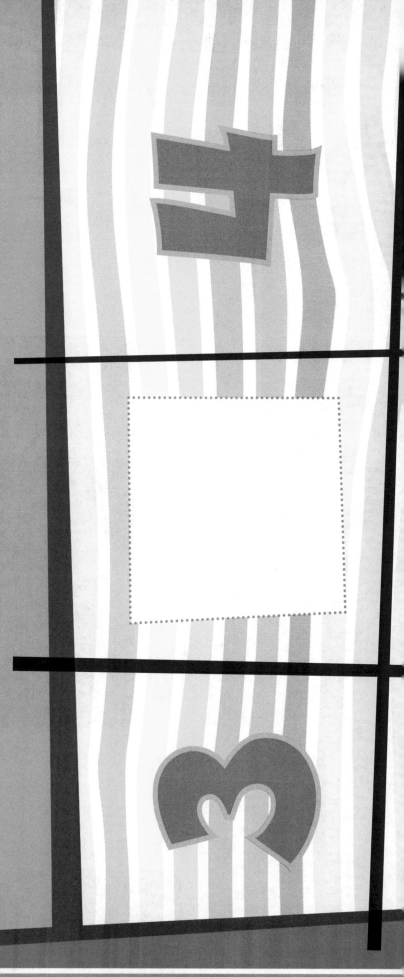

GUESS AGAIN

Write a number to answer each clue. Then, add or subtract to find the secret numbers.

How many feet do you have?

How many fingers do you have on one hand?

What is the sum?

Secret Number:

How many toes do you have?

How many ears do you have?

How many more toes than ears?

Secret Number:

Skills: Addition, Subtraction

How many eyes and noses do you have?

How many ears and mouths do you have?

What is the sum?

Secret Number:

How many sides on a square?

How many sides on a triangle?

What is the sum?

Secret Number:

PATTERN POWER

Skill: Understanding Shapes

Look at each pattern. Draw and color the shape that comes next.

e(quation)
sen+sation

Skill: Making 10

Write the missing numbers. Use numbers from the box. Use each number only once.

1	2	3	4	5	5	6	7	8	q

☐ + ☐ = 10   ☐ + ☐ = 10

☐ + ☐ = 10   ☐ + ☐ = 10

☐ + ☐ = 10

Cut out the pieces. Count the number in each group. Match the group with the number.

DARE TO DECODE

Use the code to write a number below each shape. Solve the problems. Then, draw the missing shapes.

Code Key

▲	■	▲	●	■	▲	●	■	●	▲
1	2	3	4	5	6	7	8	9	0

▲ + ● = ☐

● + ▲ = ☐☐

☐ + ☐ = ☐

☐ + ☐ = ☐

■ − ■ = ☐

● − ■ = ☐

☐ − ☐ = ☐

☐ − ☐ = ☐

Draw circles to show each number in the addition problems.

DRAW

$$14 = \begin{matrix} 10 \\ + \\ 4 \end{matrix}$$

$$12 = \begin{matrix} 10 \\ + \\ 2 \end{matrix}$$

$$18 = \begin{matrix} 10 \\ + \\ 8 \end{matrix}$$

Draw lines to connect worms that are the same length.

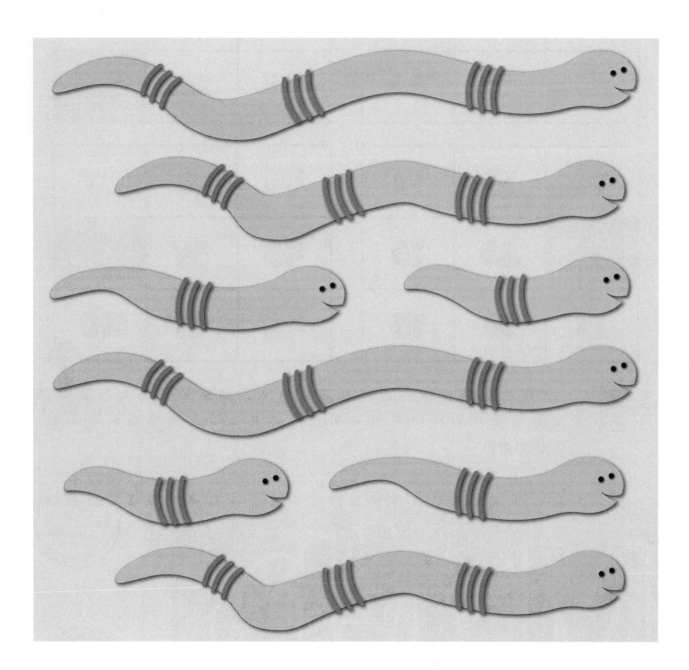

Picture Perfect!

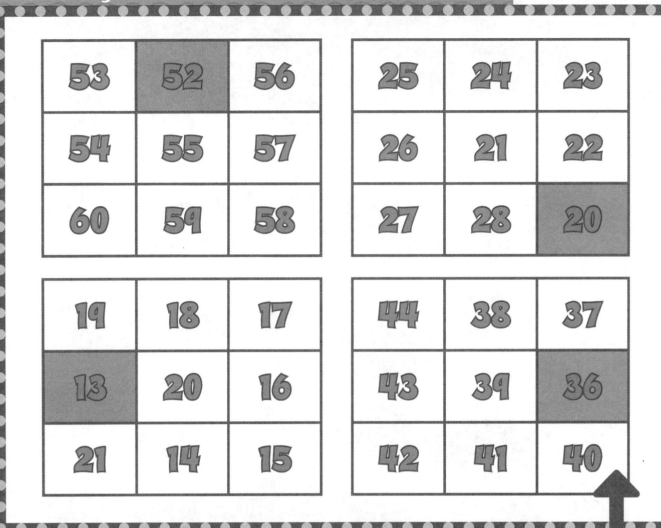

53	52	56
54	55	57
60	59	58

25	24	23
26	21	22
27	28	20

19	18	17
13	20	16
21	14	15

44	38	37
43	39	36
42	41	40

Start in the green square. Count forward. Draw a line to show your path.

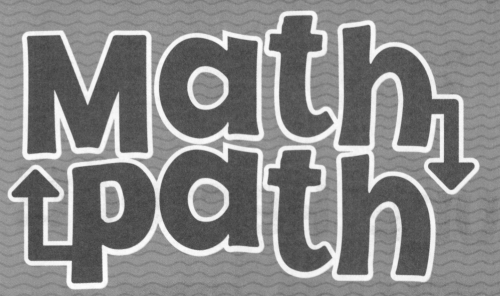

A Show of Hands

8 − 3 = 5

5 − 5 = 0

7 − 2 = 5

9 − 5 = 4

10 − 4 = 6

Cut out the pictures. Glue or tape each one under the matching subtraction problem.

Skills: Subtraction, counting

Solve the problems. Connect the dots in the order of your answers. Color the picture.

1. 3 + 2 = ☐

2. 1 + 7 = ☐

3. 2 + 4 = ☐

4. 3 + 0 = ☐

5. 3 + 6 = ☐

6. 2 + 5 = ☐

7. 1 + 3 = ☐

ON THE DOT

Skill: Addition

STORY STUMPERS

Solve the story problems. Use the pictures to help you find the answers.

Skill: Word Problems

1. Nell held up 10 fingers. She folded 3 fingers back down. How many fingers is she holding up now?

[   ] fingers

2. Mr. Ricks had 10 pears. He gave 6 pears to a friend. How many pears does he have left?

[   ] pears

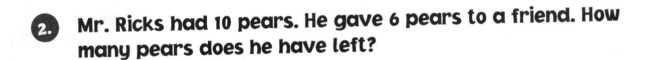

3. 10 flowers bloomed in a garden. 8 flowers were picked. How many flowers were left?

[   ] flowers

NUMBER CROSS

Skills: Addition, Subtraction

1. 9 – 5 = _____

2. 6 – 2 = _____

3. 8 – 5 = _____

4. 9 – 4 = _____

5. 10 – 6 = _____

6. 7 – 6 = _____

7. 4 – 3 = _____

8. 8 – 6 = _____

9. 9 – 3 = _____

Solve each subtraction problem. Write the answer in the puzzle. Then, find the sum of the numbers in each column and write it in the box.

SHAPE

MASTER

How many squares can
you find in the drawing?
Write the number.

Squares:

On the Lookout!

16	18	12	17	20
22	26	30	24	27
19	22	17	23	20
37	35	39	31	38
29	30	25	28	26

 12
 25
 17
 33
 20

Skill: Counting Ahead

Start with the number at the beginning of each row. Count forward 5. Circle the number you end with.

Magic Square

The sum of the numbers in each row is 9. The sum of the numbers in each column is 9. Write the missing numbers.

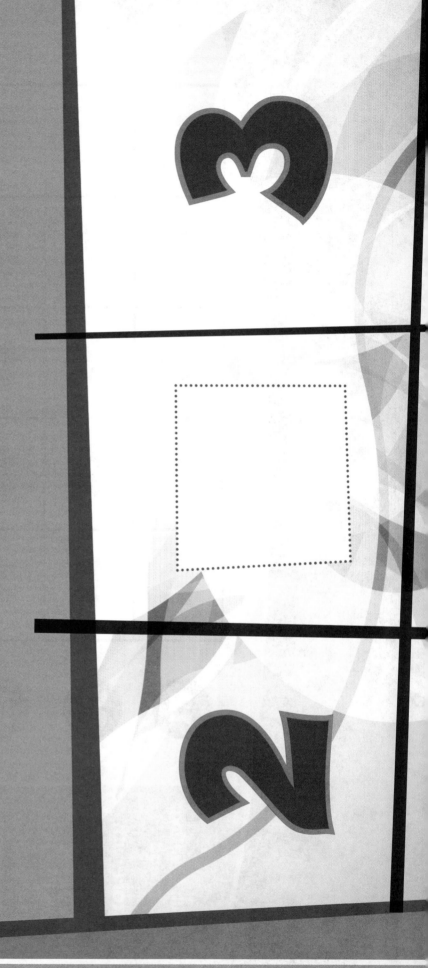

GUESS AGAIN

Read the clues.
Write each secret number.

Start at 51.

Count forward 6 more.

The secret number
is 1 less.

Secret Number:

Start at 13.

Count forward 3 more.

The secret number
is 1 more.

Secret Number:

Skill: Counting Ahead

Start at 43.

Count forward 8 more.

The secret number
is 1 less.

Secret Number:

Start at 25.

Count forward 3 more.

The secret number
is 1 more.

Secret Number:

Skills: Comparing Groups, Counting

Cut out the puzzle pieces. Fit them together so that equal groups are side-by-side.

e(quation)
sen+sation

Each picture has replaced a number. Use what you know about doubles. Write the number for each picture.

🐚 + 🐚 = 8   🐚 = ⬚

🍑 + 🍑 = 4   🍑 = ⬚

🐓 + 🐓 = 6   🐓 = ⬚

🥪 + 🥪 = 10   🥪 = ⬚

🐋 + 🐋 = 2   🐋 = ⬚

PATTERN POWER

10	20	30		50
20				
	40		60	
40				80
				90

Look at the pattern in each row and column. Write the missing numbers. Hint: Each number you write will end with 0.

DARE TO DECODE

Use what you know about subtraction to crack the code.

Code Key

$10 -$ $= 3$ $-$ $= 5$

$10 -$ $= 6$ $6 -$ $=$

 $-$ $= 6$ $-$ $= 1$

Draw a line from each solid shape to a flat shape that matches one of its faces.

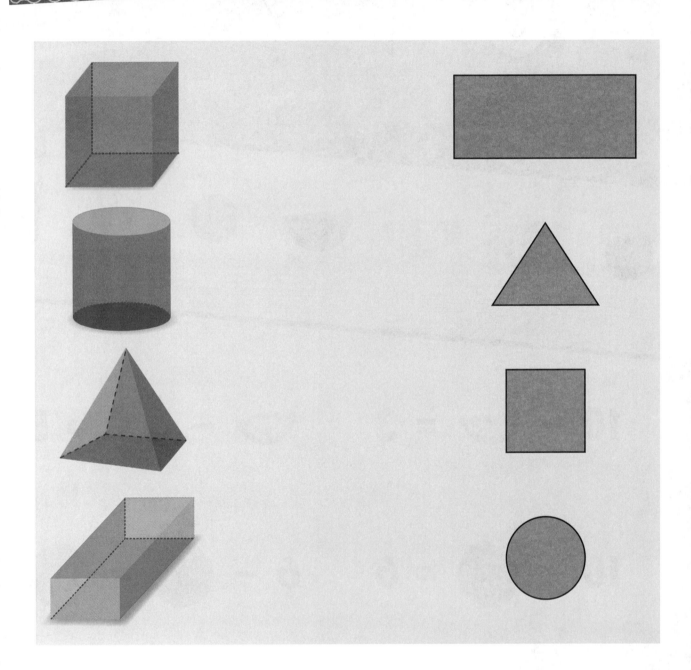

Picture Perfect!

Read each number. Draw and color that many shapes.

DRAW

Skills: Counting, Drawing Shapes

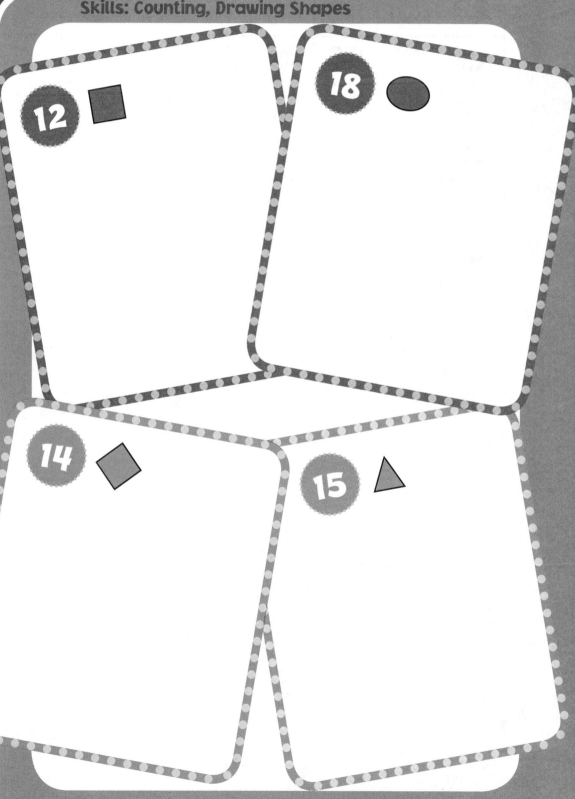

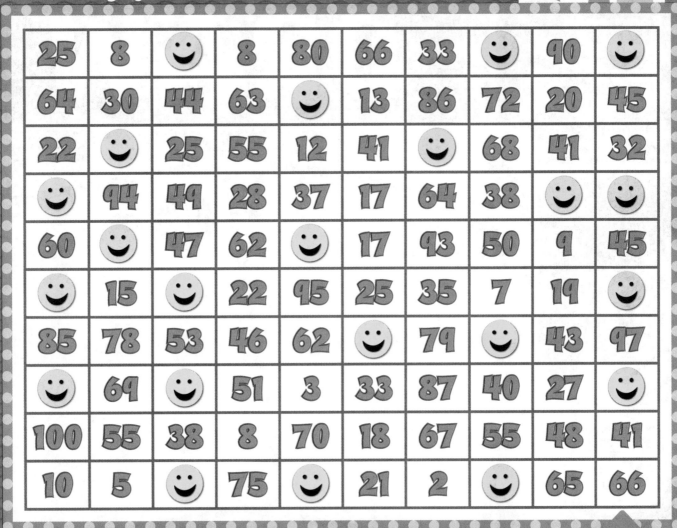

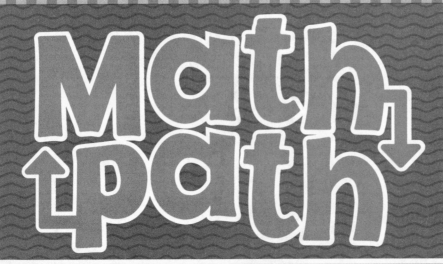

Start at 10. Draw a line to 20. Keep drawing lines as you count by tens to 100. How many smiley faces did you pass? Write the number.

Smiley Faces: ☐

A Show of Hands

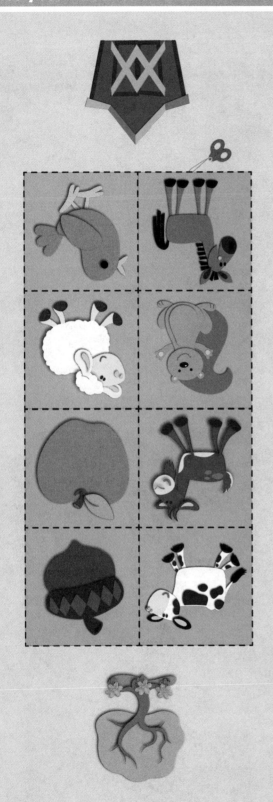

Cut out each picture. Glue
or tape it next to the place
where it might be found.

Skill: Classifying

Solve the subtraction problems. Connect the dots in the order of your answers. Color the picture.

1. $10 - 6 =$ ☐

2. $9 - 3 =$ ☐

3. $8 - 7 =$ ☐

4. $5 - 3 =$ ☐

5. $10 - 2 =$ ☐

6. $9 - 4 =$ ☐

7. $8 - 1 =$ ☐

8. $10 - 7 =$ ☐

ON THE DOT

Skill: Subtraction

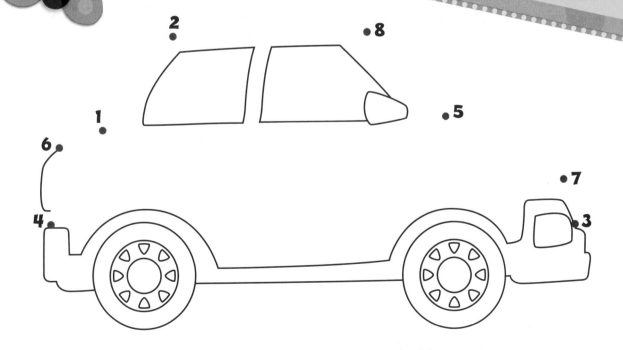

STORY STUMPERS

Solve the story problems. Use the pictures to help you find the answers.

Skill: Word Problems

1. 3 clouds in the sky looked like boats. 4 clouds looked like fish. How many clouds looked like boats and fish?

_____ clouds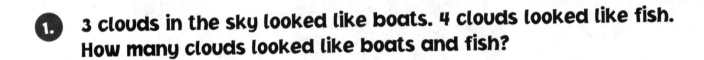

2. 6 snails hid under a leaf. 3 more snails crawled under the leaf. How many snails in all were under the leaf?

_____ snails

3. Max counted 5 shooting stars. Then, he counted 2 more. How many shooting stars did Max count in all?

_____ shooting stars

SHAPE MASTER

Draw a picture using only circles and squares.

NUMBER CROSS

Skills: Addition, Subtraction

1. 8 − 6 = _____

2. 9 − 3 = _____

3. 8 − 3 = _____

4. 10 − 6 = _____

5. 7 − 5 = _____

6. 4 − 1 = _____

7. 10 − 9 = _____

8. 6 − 5 = _____

9. 10 − 8 = _____

Solve each subtraction problem. Write the answer in the puzzle. Then, find the sum of the numbers in each column and write it in the box.

Skill: Understanding Shapes

Cut out the puzzle pieces. Fit them together to make one circle, one square, and one triangle.

IT FITS!

GUESS AGAIN

Read the clues.
Write the secret numbers.

Start with 3.

Add 2 more.

Take away 1.

Secret Number:

Start with 9.

Take away 4.

Add 2 more.

Secret Number:

Skills: Addition, Subtraction

Start with 7.

Add 2 more.

Take away 6.

Secret Number:

Start with 10.

Take away 5.

Add 1 more.

Secret Number:

Magic Square

Add up the yummy rows and columns using the code. Write the sums in the blanks.

= 3

= 1

= 4

= 2

On the Lookout!

9	5	11	16
14	17	6	15
7	12	20	8
19	10	18	13

Skill: Counting

Find and circle the numbers in the puzzle that tell how many items are in each group.

Each domino on the left has 10 dots. Draw a line to the domino that will make the number of dots shown.

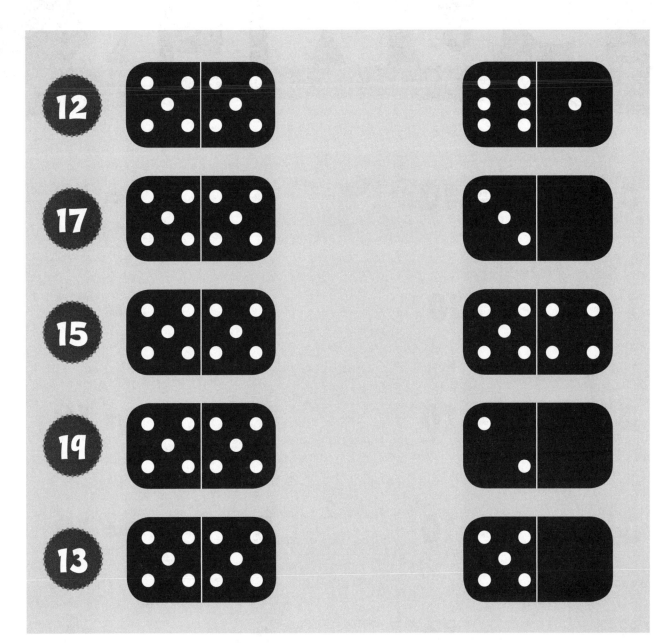

Picture Perfect!

PATTERN POWER

$0 + \boxed{} = 10$ $\qquad$ $5 + \boxed{} = 10$

$1 + \boxed{} = 10$ $\qquad$ $6 + \boxed{} = 10$

$2 + \boxed{} = 10$ $\qquad$ $7 + \boxed{} = 10$

$3 + \boxed{} = 10$ $\qquad$ $8 + \boxed{} = 10$

$4 + \boxed{} = 10$ $\qquad$ $9 + \boxed{} = 10$

Write the missing numbers in the addition problems.
Do you see the pattern?

e(quation)
sen+sation

Write the missing number in each subtraction problem.

$9 - \boxed{} = 6$

$\boxed{} - 3 = 2$

$\boxed{} - 1 = 7$

$6 - \boxed{} = 1$

$7 - \boxed{} = 5$

$\boxed{} - 3 = 5$

$9 - \boxed{} = 2$

$\boxed{} - 4 = 3$

DARE TO DECODE

Use the addition problems to crack the code. One number is given for you.

Code Key

●	◆	■	▲	⬡ (circle)	⬡ (hexagon)	★
				10		

● + ■ = 15   ● + ◆ = 12

● + ● = 14   ● + ⬡ = 18

● + ▲ = 11   ● + ★ = 19

A Show of Hands

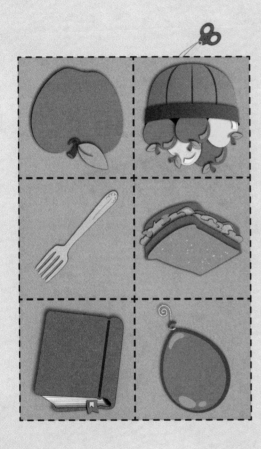

Skill: Comparing Weight

Cut out the items. Glue or tape them onto the scales to make each picture true.

STORY STUMPERS

Solve the story problems. Use the pictures to help you find the answers.

Skills: Word Problems, Place Value

1. There were 10 crabs on the beach. 3 more crabs came out of the water and onto the beach. How many crabs are on the beach now?

☐ ☐ crabs

2. Dad baked 10 cookies on one tray. On another tray, he baked 6 cookies. How many cookies did Dad bake in all?

☐ ☐ cookies

3. During the first half of the game, the team hit 10 baseballs. During the second half, the team hit 8 baseballs. How many baseballs did the team hit during the game?

☐ ☐ baseballs

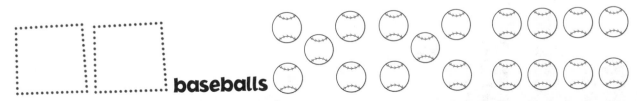

Shapes are all around you. Look around the room, out the window, or outside. Find an example of each shape. Draw what you see.

DRAW

QUICK

Skill: Drawing Shapes

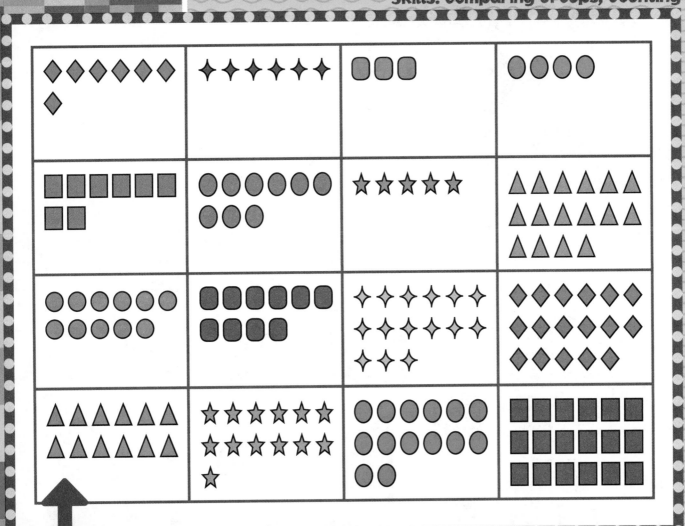

Start in the space with the smallest group. Draw a line to the space with one more. Keep going until you reach the largest group.

Math path

SHAPE

Skills: Understanding Shapes, Classifying, Counting

Count the shapes. Write a number to tell how many of each you see. Then, count the colors. Write a number to tell how many of each you see.

pink =

▷ =

blue =

■ =

orange =

○ =

NUMBER CROSS

1. 5 − 4 = _____

2. 2 + 6 = _____

3. 10 − 5 = _____

Grid cells numbered: 1, 4, 2, 7, 5, 3, 8, 6, 9

4. 7 − 4 = _____

5. 4 − 3 = _____

6. 9 − 6 = _____

7. 5 + 1 = _____

8. 10 − 9 = _____

9. 7 − 5 = _____

Solve each problem. Write the answer in the puzzle. Then, find the sum of the numbers in each column and write it in the box.

Write a number to tell how many stars are in each group. Then, draw lines to connect groups that are the same. Write the name of the shape you made.

ON THE DOT

Skills: Comparing Groups, Counting, Comparing Numbers

Shape: _____

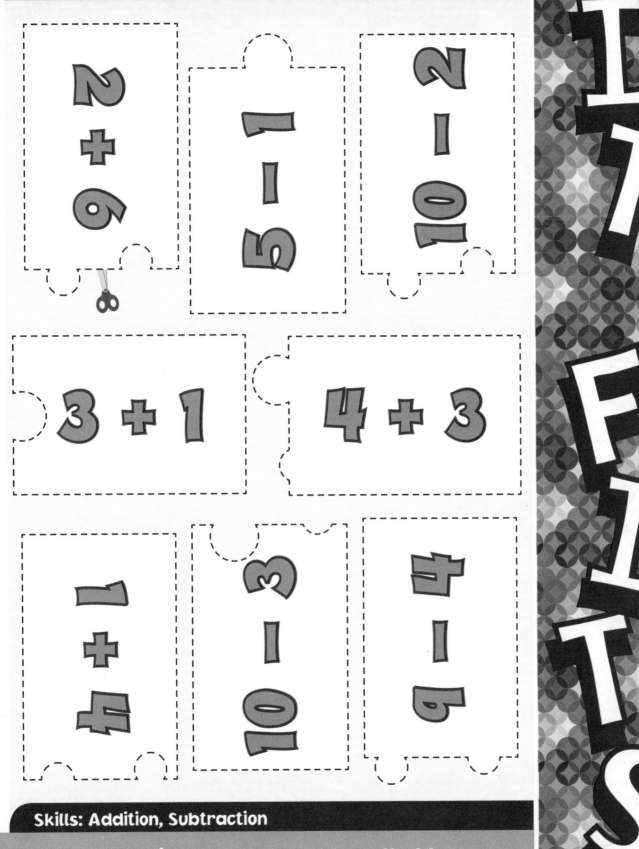

ITS FITS!

Skills: Addition, Subtraction

Cut out the pieces. Match problems that have the same answers.

GUESS AGAIN

Read the clues.
Write each secret number.

Start with 10 ones.

How many sides are on a triangle?

Add that many ones.

Secret Number:

Start with 10 ones.

How many days are in a week?

Add that many ones.

Secret Number:

Skill: Place Value

Start with 10 ones.

How many fingers are on one hand?

Add that many ones.

Secret Number:

Start with 10 ones.

How many arms does an octopus have?

Add that many ones.

Secret Number:

Magic Square

Write the numbers 1 to 9 in the magic square. Follow this rule: From top to bottom, and from left to right, the numbers must go from greatest to least.

1 2 3 4 5 6 7 8 9

On the Lookout!

5	11	18	7
9	20	13	19
12	16	6	15
17	8	14	10

Skill: Counting

Find and circle the numbers in the puzzle that tell how many items are in each group.

e(quation) sen+sation

These problems are missing their signs!
Write +, −, or = in each square.

8 □ 3 □ 5

2 □ 2 □ 4

4 □ 1 □ 5

8 □ 4 □ 4

10 □ 5 □ 5

7 □ 1 □ 8

5 □ 4 □ 9

9 □ 7 □ 2

PATTERN POWER

| 20 | 30 | ☐ | 50 | ☐ |

| ☐ | 50 | 60 | ☐ | 80 |

| 10 | ☐ | 30 | ☐ | 50 |

| ☐ | 60 | ☐ | 80 | 90 |

| ☐ | 70 | 80 | ☐ | 100 |

Find the pattern in each row. Write the missing numbers.
Hint: Each number you write will end in 0.

The first jar in each row has 10 jelly beans. Draw jelly beans in the second jar to make the number shown.

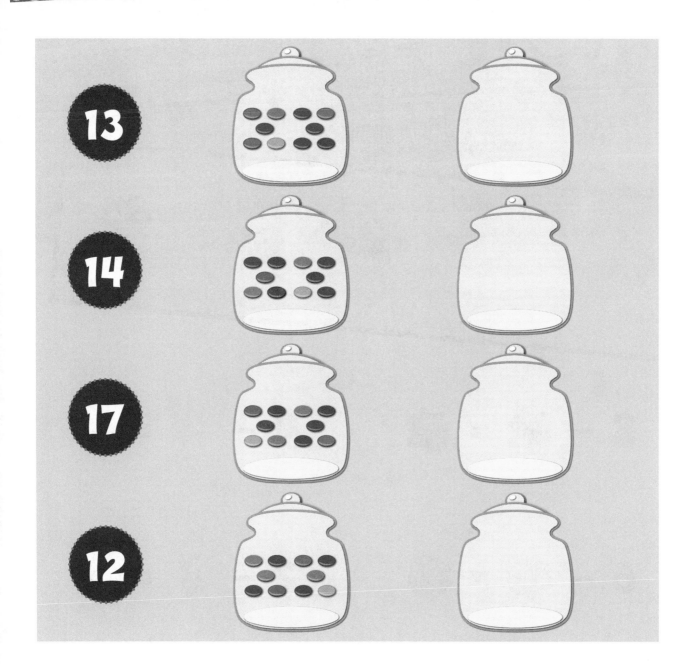

Picture Perfect!

DARE TO DECODE

Skill: Subtraction

Each picture has replaced a number. Use what you know about doubles to crack the code. Write a number below each picture in the key.

Code Key

8 – =

4 – =

6 – =

2 – =

10 – =

A Show of Hands

Inside

How many?

Outside

How many?

Skills: Counting, classifying

Cut out each picture. Does it show something you usually find inside or something you usually find outside? Glue or tape each picture where it belongs. Write a number to tell how many are in each group.

STORY STUMPERS

Solve the story problems. Draw Xs on the pictures to help you find the answers.

1. There are 10 balloons in a bunch. Four of the balloons pop. How many balloons are left in the bunch?

[ ] balloons

2. There were 9 ladybugs on a mailbox. Six of the ladybugs flew away. How many ladybugs were left on the mailbox?

[ ] ladybugs

3. Seven pizzas were ordered for a party. Five of the pizzas were eaten. How many pizzas were left over?

[ ] pizzas

Draw polka dots on the triangle. Draw stripes on the square. Draw a face on the circle.

DRAW

QUICK

Skill: Understanding Shapes

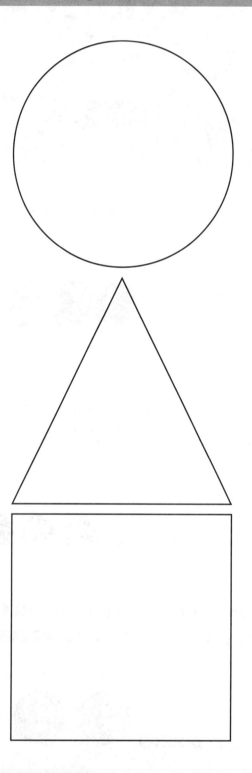

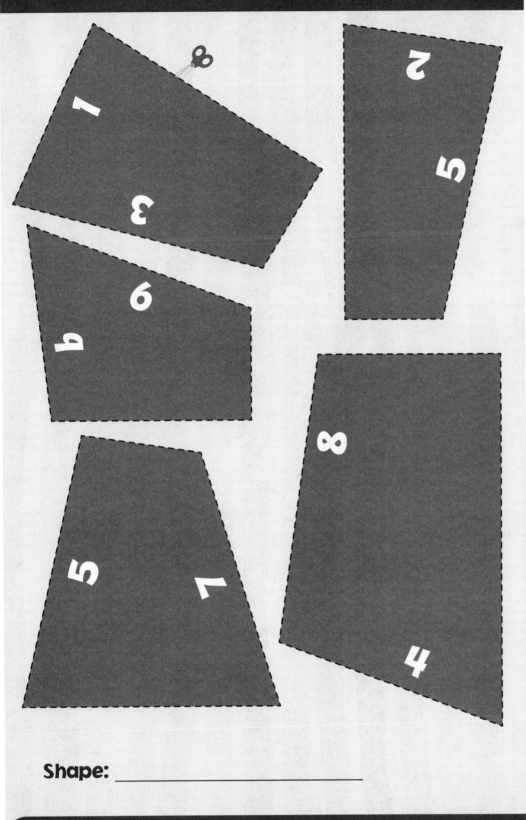

Shape: _____

Skills: Making 10, Understanding Shapes

Cut out the puzzle pieces. Find the numbers that add to 10. Put them next to each other. Write the name of the shape you made.

Skills: Counting, Comparing Numbers

NUMBER CROSS

1. 

2. 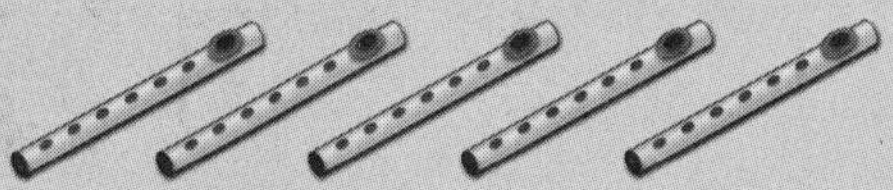

3. 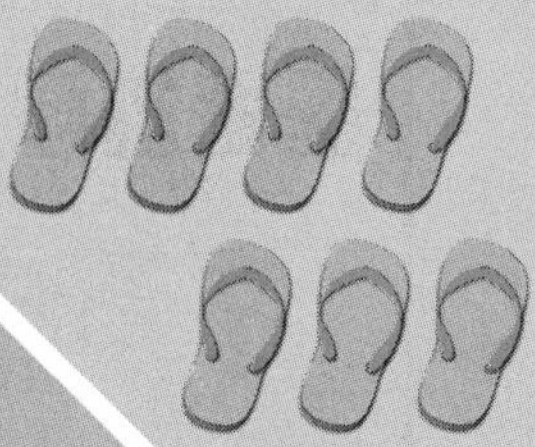

1
10
4
2
7
5
3
8
6
9

4. 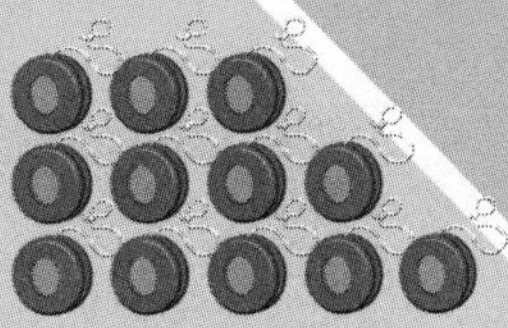

5. 

6. 

7. 

8. 

9. 

Count the items in each group. Write the number in the puzzle. Circle the biggest number you wrote. Cross out the smallest number. One is done for you.

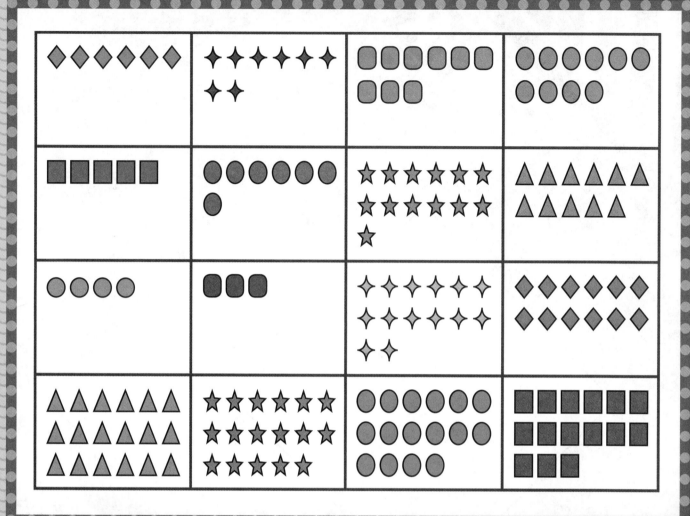

Start in the space with the smallest group. Draw a line to the space with one more. Keep going until you reach the largest group.

Math path

LANGUAGE ARTS

WORD MATH

Write a word to solve each puzzle.

1. l +  − fr = _____

2. b + − r = _____

3. c + − b = _____

4. w + 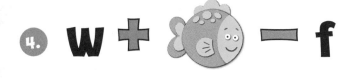 − f

= _____

5. w + − n = _____

6. c + 🧹 − r

= _____

In Search Of

Find and circle these words in the puzzle:

yes
too
ran
saw
four
get
soon
new

Q H U O
L C W D F O U R
X Y J Q V D M X
Q P V S F D P Z J
J X Z X M Q R L Q F
E A M M P V Y G E T F M R H
B V H X B G T Z Z V P Y E S V M N E W V
Q M Z S A W V S O O N H S O H J N L F T U
R T W P X E O E V A Z Z Q M Y N T Y Z K O Q
Q Q R V T O O G C G Q N A H G X T N J J I V
H B L B N L O C S V D O Y F X L G R A N P W
H H J P E B U I F O O Y Z Y Y F H T U M O M
A L M R X S Y G J K Q L M X D B J X T R
I A B C L T P D
E B E R

Skill: Sight Words

smile

small

day

down

Skill: Opposites

IN PIECES

Cut out the pieces. Match words and pictures that are opposites.

big

frown

up

night

CODE BREAKER

Skill: Spelling

Use the code to write words.

1.

_____ _____ _____

2.

_____ _____ _____

3.

_____ _____ _____ _____

4.

_____ _____ _____ _____

Code Key

a	c	e	f	h	k	n	s	t	u

MAZE CRAZE

Skill: Short Vowel Sounds

Help the sheep find a path to the barn. Color each word that has a short vowel sound. Choose words you colored to write on the lines.

rip	sheep	kite	rope
dog	ice	pane	pool
bell	bug	net	mine
rake	note	duck	peek
spoon	seen	pan	lip

short a:

_____

short e:

_____

short i:

_____

short o:

_____

short u:

_____

Sentence Scramble

Draw a line to connect the words and make a sentence. Write the sentence on the lines. Add capital letters where they are needed. Use an end mark at the end of the sentence.

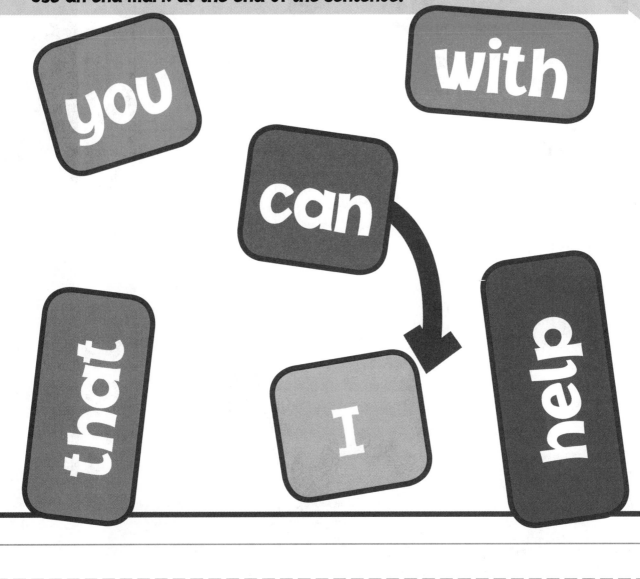

_____

_____

_____

_____

_____

JUMBLED UP

Skills: Consonant Sounds, Spelling

The first letter of each word is in the wrong place. Find the letter. Then, write the word that matches the picture.

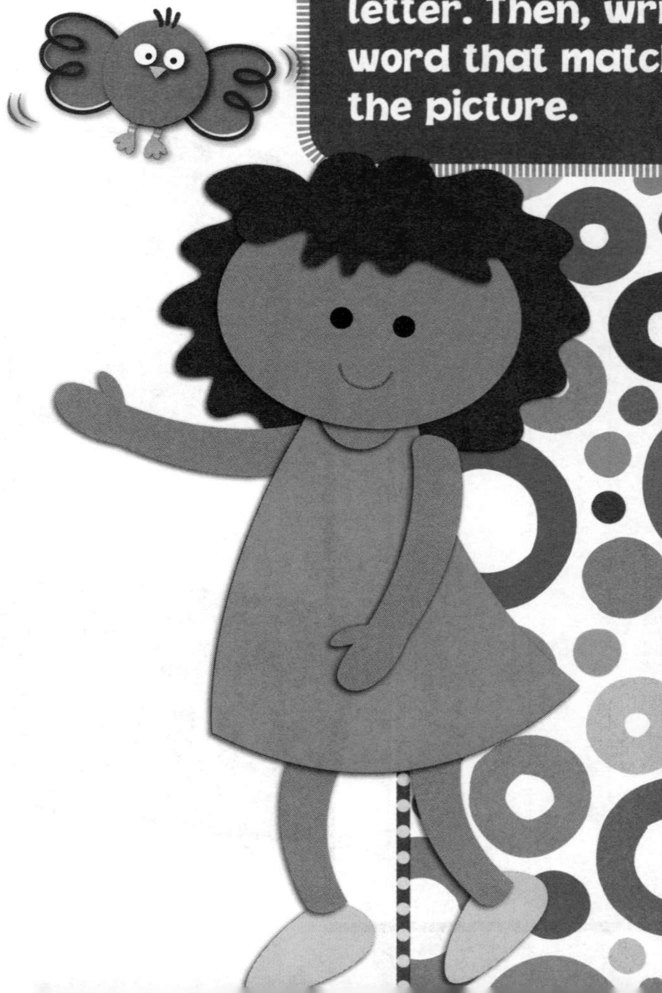

1. 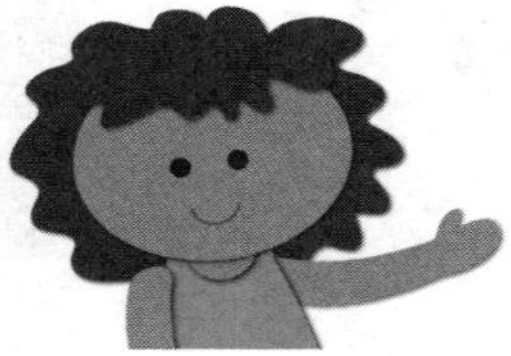 irgl ____________

2. 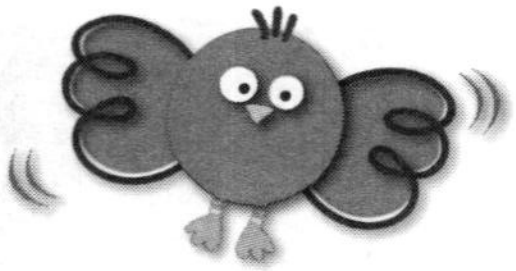 irdb ____________

3. 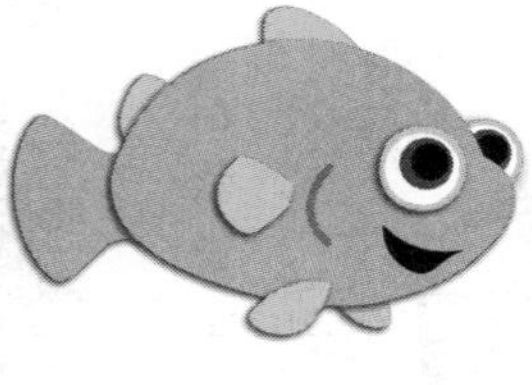 isfh ____________

4. 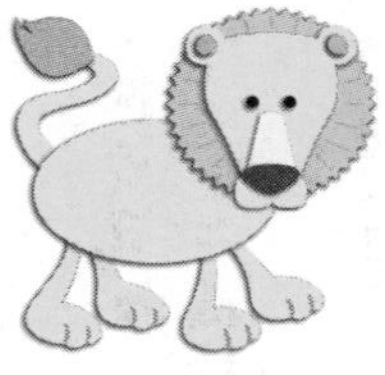 ionl ____________

5. 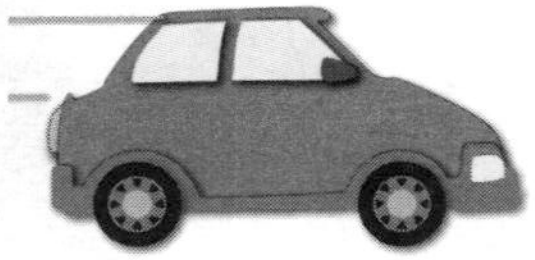 acr ____________

Skill: Classifying

Cut out the pictures. Look at each one. If it shows something that belongs in the ocean, glue or tape it on the page.

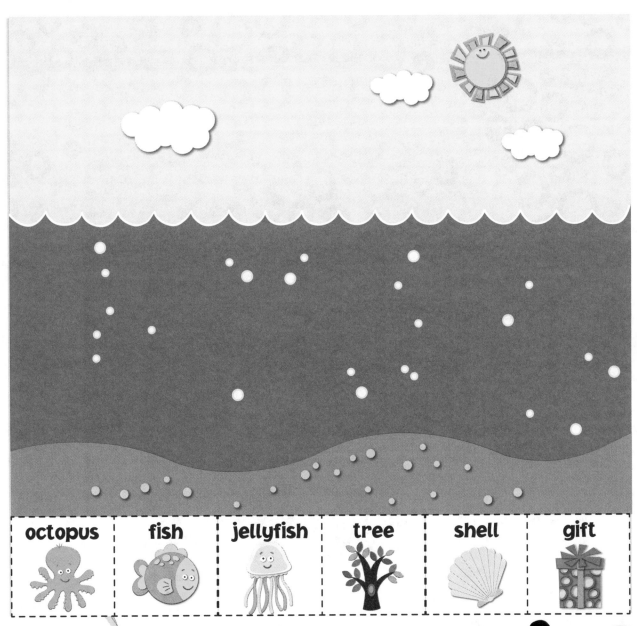

octopus | fish | jellyfish | tree | shell | gift

Picture This!

Skill: Nouns

Fill in the chart. Write a noun that begins with each letter shown. You may use the nouns shown in the box or use other nouns you know. One is done for you.

sun log web bib duck ant

Letters	Nouns
s	
b	
l	
d	duck
a	
w	

CODE BREAKER

Use the code to answer the questions.

_____

_ _ _ _

1. What letter comes after "g"? _____

2. What letter comes between "h"

_____

_ _ _ _

and "p"? _____

3. Write the uppercase form of the letter

_____

_ _ _ _

between "m" and "E." _____

_____

_ _ _ _

4. What letter comes before "B"? _____

5. Write the uppercase form of the letter

_____

_ _ _ _

that comes after "y." _____

6. What letter comes between "G"

_____

_ _ _ _

and "I"? _____

Skills: Handwriting, Letter Recognition

Code Key

D	G	h	I	P	k	L	Q	b	B	g	y	m	a	E

MIRROR
MIRROR

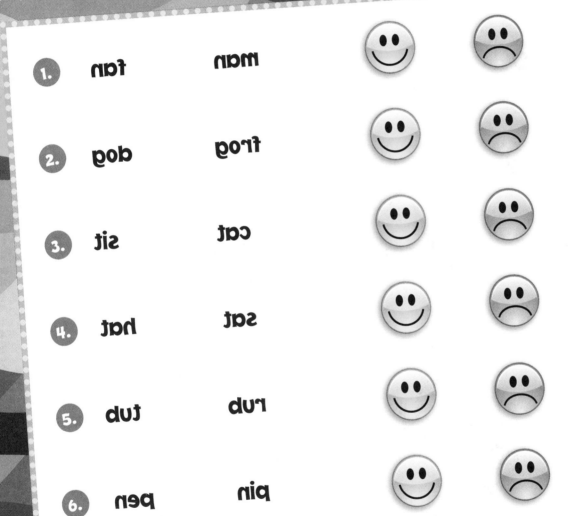

1. fan   man   :) :(

2. dog   frog   :) :(

3. sit   cat   :) :(

4. hat   sat   :) :(

5. tub   rub   :) :(

6. pen   pin   :) :(

Hold this page up to a mirror to read each set of words. Do they rhyme? If they do, circle the smiley face (:)). If they do not, circle the sad face (:().

121

Not Your Usual Workbook · Kindergarten

RIDDLE ME

Write a letter for each clue. Put the letters together to spell a word with a prefix that means "not." Write more words with the prefix.

Skills: Prefixes, Consonant Sounds

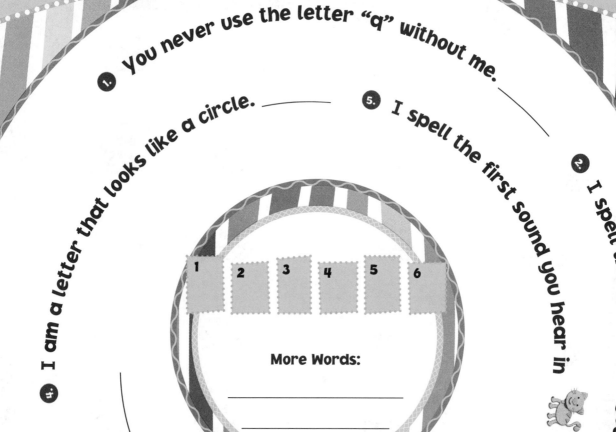

1. You never use the letter "q" without me. _____

5. I spell the first sound you hear in _____

2. I spell the first sound you hear in _____

4. I am a letter that looks like a circle. _____

3. I spell the first sound you hear in _____

6. I spell the last sound you hear in _____

| 1 | 2 | 3 | 4 | 5 | 6 |

More Words:

_____

_____

In Search Of

Skill: Question Words

Find and circle these question words:

who
what
where
when
why
how

S J
G Z Q V
E N D X R V
M M X R J B X X
L T M H O W D L Q T
K D E E J O K O L N S O
Y M W H O V B R R Q P K I Y
N F A Z H P W H E R E W H E N B
Z Q C Z Y X U W H A T R G W Q Z E A
D T A R G P V X D F P C F A D N B E K M
K Q W U S I R C D N Q R Z C J X S B D Y
Q E M F V Z F X I X X S M X X F K A
W E V V Y F P B L B M G I N U A
Y B A O Z P P D W H Y J O J
W T X E A G O R Y K W P
I G W O N X C A F K
Z F G U Q R H E
N P X E I Q
W K U I
I M

Skill: Spelling

GO ON ACROSS

Name each picture. Write the name in the puzzle.

1.

2.

3.

Write the letters that are in circles. Draw a picture to show the word you made.

Sudoku for you

Skill: Spelling

Write letters in the boxes so that each row and column has the letters to spell

☀ sun

Do not use any letter more than once in the same row or column.

U		
		S
S	U	

Skills: Verbs, Letter Recognition

Cross out the letters of the alphabet in order. The letters that are left will spell four verbs. Write them on the lines.

j	u	m	p	a	b	c
d	e	f	g	h	i	j
k	b	a	k	e	l	m
n	o	p	q	r	s	t
k	i	c	k	u	v	w
x	y	z	f	a	l	l

Skill: Consonant Sounds

Cut out the pictures. Say the name of each one. Glue or tape each picture under the number word that has the same beginning sound.

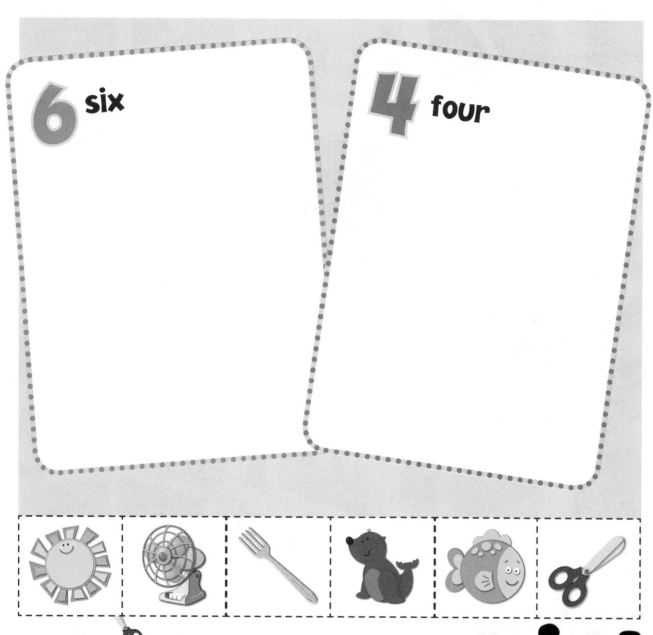

Picture This!

1. Take away the bottom line of "E." What letter do you have?

_____

_ _ _ _ _ _ _

_____

2. What letter is shaped like a smile?

_____

_ _ _ _ _ _ _

_____

3. Take away the cross line of "A." Turn it upside down. What letter do you have?

_____

_ _ _ _ _ _ _

_____

4. What letter looks like one rung of a ladder?

_____

_ _ _ _ _ _ _

_____

5. Turn "M" upside down. What letter do you have?

_____

_ _ _ _ _ _ _

_____

How well do you know your letters? It is time to find out! Write an uppercase letter to answer each question.

Letter Box

H	V
F	U
W	

Skills: Handwriting, Letter Recognition

QUIZ WHIZ

PRESTO

Skill: Rhyming Words

Look at the first word. Change one letter to write a rhyming word that matches the picture clue.

cat

van

log

red

man

car

CHANGE-O!

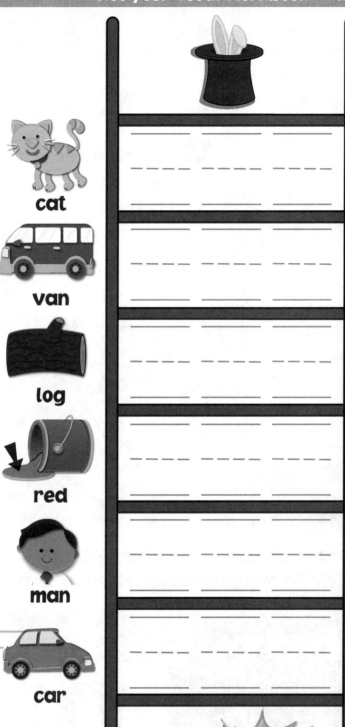

Unscramble each word inside a house. Write the words to finish the story.

 rea

 ylpa

 reThe

 hTye

 omec

_____ _____ at

cats _____ _____ want to

my door. _____ _____ inside to

_____ _____ .

GO ON ACROSS

Say the name of each picture. Write it in the puzzle.

Hint: All the words rhyme.

1.
2.
3.

Write the letters that are in circles. Draw a picture to show the word you made.

A bat eats bugs.

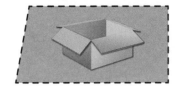

Use the bat to hit the ball.

A fly buzzed by.

IN PIECES

Cut out the pieces. Match each sentence with a picture that shows the meaning of the word shown in white.

We will fly to New York.

Put tape on the box.

Dad likes to box with Max.

Sentence Scramble

Draw a line to connect the words and make a sentence. Write the sentence on the lines. Add capital letters where they are needed. Use an end mark at the end of the sentence.

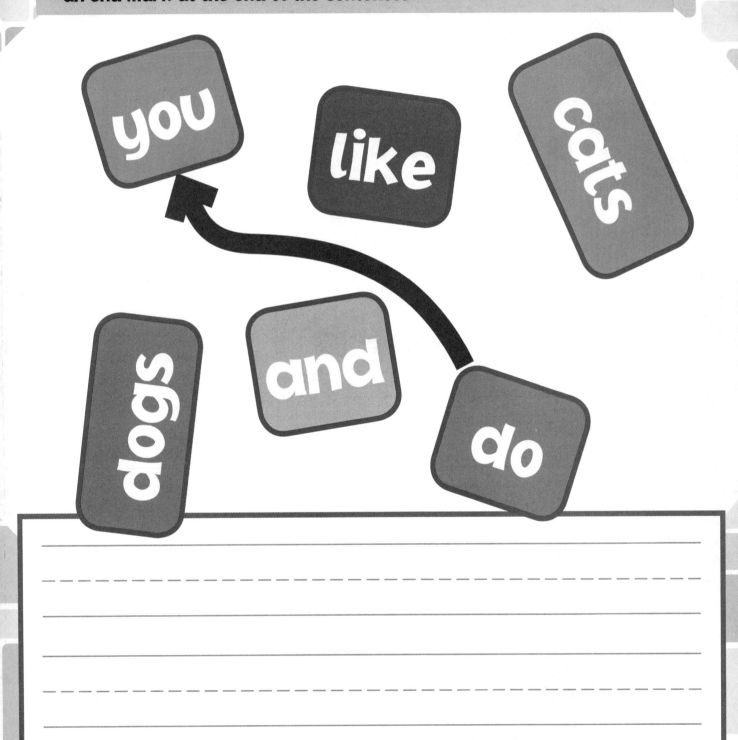

Write the word that solves each puzzle. Then, add "s" or "es" to make the word plural.

S or es

1. j + 🚗 − c =

_____   _____
- - - - - - - - -   - - - - - - - - -
_____   _____

    one   more than one

2. h + 🐱 − c =

_____   _____
- - - - - - - - -   - - - - - - - - -
_____   _____

    one   more than one

3. f + 📦 − b =

_____   _____
- - - - - - - - -   - - - - - - - - -
_____   _____

    one   more than one

4.  − r =

_____   _____
_ _ _ _ _ _ _ _ _ _ _   _ _ _ _ _ _ _ _ _ _ _
_____   _____
one   more than one

5. r + 🐞 − b =

_____   _____
_ _ _ _ _ _ _ _ _ _ _   _ _ _ _ _ _ _ _ _ _ _
_____   _____
one   more than one

6. h + ✒ − p =

_____   _____
_ _ _ _ _ _ _ _ _ _ _   _ _ _ _ _ _ _ _ _ _ _
_____   _____
one   more than one

Look at each letter. Does it have straight lines, curvy lines, or both? Write the letters in the Venn diagram.

A Q c M d f o I R S k j

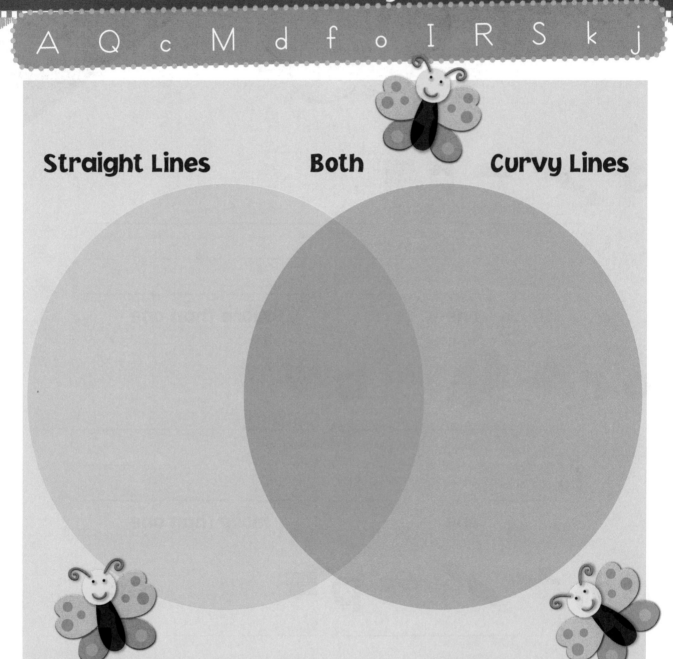

Straight Lines   **Both**   **Curvy Lines**

Picture This!

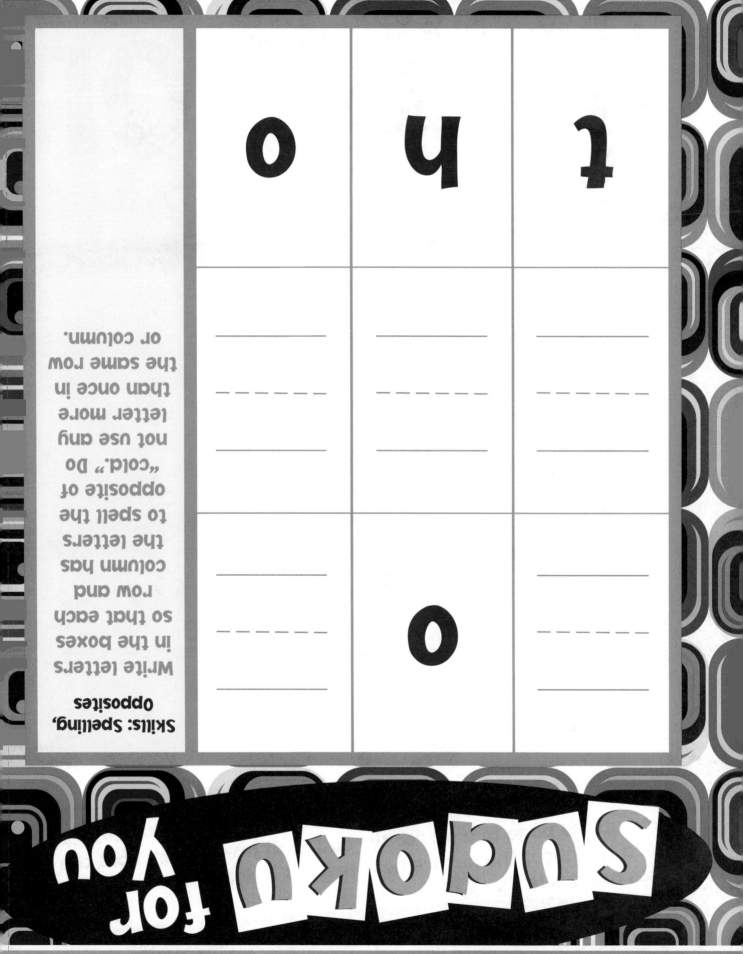

	o	h	t
			o

Skills: Spelling, Opposites

Write letters in the boxes so that each row and column has the letters to spell the opposite of "cold." Do not use any letter more than once in the same row or column.

Sudoku for You

MIRROR

1. in 👍 👎

2. on 👍 👎

3. under  👍 👎

4. beside 👍 👎

5. between  👍 👎

6. over 👍 👎

Hold up the page to a mirror to read each preposition. Does the word tell about the picture next to it? If it does, circle 👍. If it does not, circle 👎.

CODE BREAKER

Skill: Short Vowel Sounds

Use the code to find the letter that completes each short vowel word. Write the word on the line.

1. h ⚽ d = _____

2. g 🎾 m = _____

3. h 🎾 g = _____

4. t 🏏 p = _____

5. m ⚾ n = _____

6. j ⚽ m = _____

Code Key

a	e	i	o	u
⚽	⚾	🏏	🎾	🎾

Say the names of the pictures on each flower. What letter makes their starting sound? Write it in the center of the flower.

10

Picture This!

1. I am the opposite of "white."
What am I?

_ _ _ _ _ _ _ _ _

2. My long o sound is spelled
the same as in "moon."
What am I?

_ _ _ _ _ _ _ _ _

3. I rhyme with "hill."
What am I?

_ _ _ _ _ _ _ _ _

4. Start with "same." Change
the first letter to "c."
What am I?

_ _ _ _ _ _ _ _ _

5. I am the opposite of "he."
What am I?

_ _ _ _ _ _ _ _ _

Use the clues to answer each question. Choose words
from the word box.

Word Box

she	black
will	came
soon	

Skill: Sight Words

QUIZ WHIZ

In Search Of

Read the first word in each row. Circle one letter that could take the place of the orange letter to make a rhyming word. Write the rhyming word on the line.

hat   b   c   f   m   r

dig   b   f   j   p   w

mop   c   h   p   t   b

rot   c   d   g   h   n

tug   b   d   h   j   m

lip   d   h   r   s   z

GO ON ACROSS

Say the name of each picture. In the puzzle, write the letter that makes its beginning sound. Then, read the word formed in each row. Color the picture that matches.

1.

2.

3.

4.

5.

6.

ALPHA-
CHALLENGE

Not Your Usual Workbook · **Kindergarten**

IN PIECES

Cut out the pieces. Match each suffix with a base word to complete the butterflies.

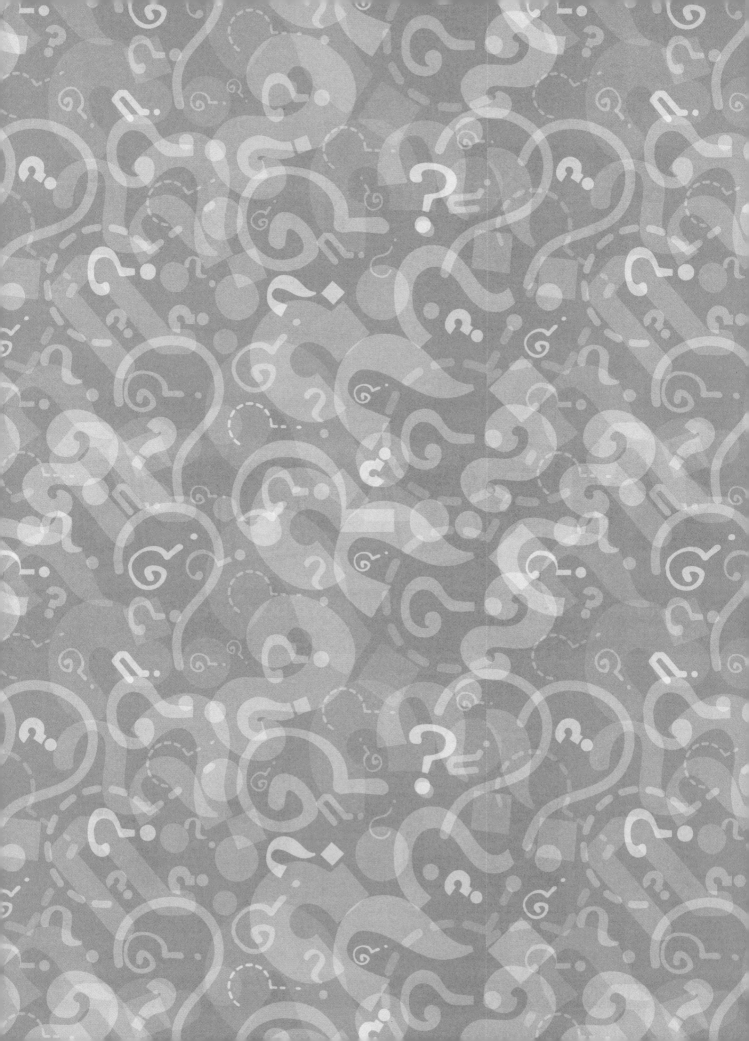

Look at each picture. Unscramble the letters to write a word with an opposite meaning.

1. **rotsh**

2. **oby**

3. **flul**

4. **olcd**

5. **ndeur**

PRESTO

Skill: Long and Short Vowel Sounds

Read each word with a long vowel sound. Cross out one letter. Write the new word that has a short vowel sound. Use the picture clues to help you.

cane

bead

coat

boat

pine

neat

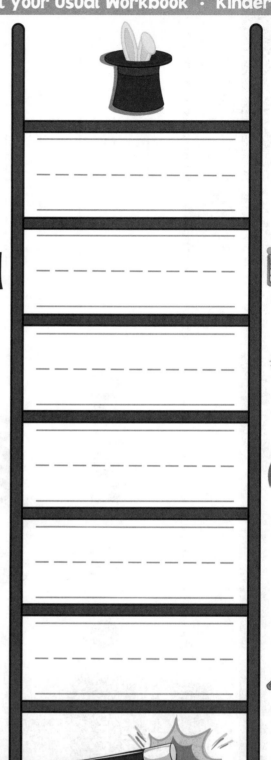

CHANGE-O!

Sentence Scramble

Draw a line to connect the words and make a sentence. Write the sentence on the lines. Add capital letters where they are needed. Use an end mark at the end of the sentence.

Sudoku for You

Skill: Spelling

Write letters in the boxes so that each row and column has the letters to spell 🐜. Do not use any letter more than once in the same row or column.

a	t	
n		
		a

152   Not Your Usual Workbook · Kindergarten

Skill: Sight Words

Help the polar bear find the igloo. Color each word that starts with "w" to make a path. On the lines, write four words you know that begin with "w."

want	good	out	no
was	well	went	how
have	that	what	who
did	too	all	with
be	she	new	will

1. small   green   _____

2. fuzzy   sweet   _____

3. salty   brown   _____

4. loud   grumpy   _____

5. dark   cozy   _____

Read each set of words. What do they make you think of? Write a word or phrase that comes to mind. Use the example to help you.

Example
new   red

my bike

Skill: Vocabulary

QUIZ WHIZ

PREST-O CHANGE-O!

Skill: Long and Short Vowel Sounds

Read each word with a long vowel sound. Cross out one letter. Write the new word that has a short vowel sound. Use the picture clues to help you.

tube

pain

care

read

beat

hate

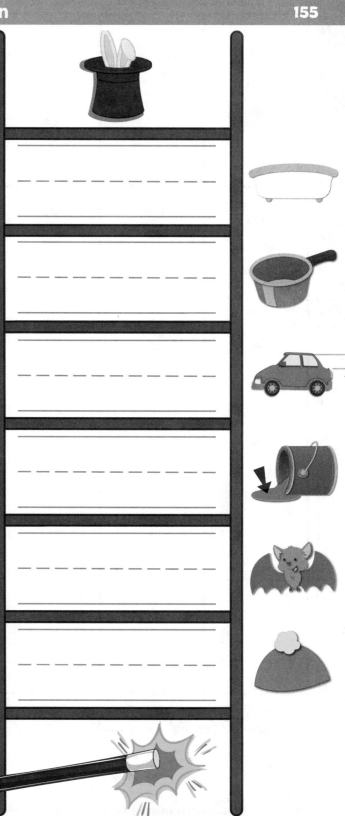

Skills: Classifying, Consonant Sounds
Read the categories and examples. For each category, write another example that begins with the letter shown. The first one is done for you.

Shapes	circle	oval	triangle
Toys	train	ball	d _ _ _ _ _ _
Foods	salad	yogurt	s _ _ _ _ _ _
Number Words	two	six	f _ _ _ _ _ _
Animals	dog	lion	r _ _ _ _ _ _

ALPHA-
CHALLENGE

Unscramble each verb and write it on the line. Then, draw a line from each verb to the picture that shows the action.

1. **hpo**

2. **wsmi**

3. **nru**

4. **gsni**

5. **ltme**

RIDDLE ME

Write a letter for each clue. Put the letters together to write a word with a suffix that means "the most." Write more words with the suffix.

Skills: Suffixes, Consonant Sounds

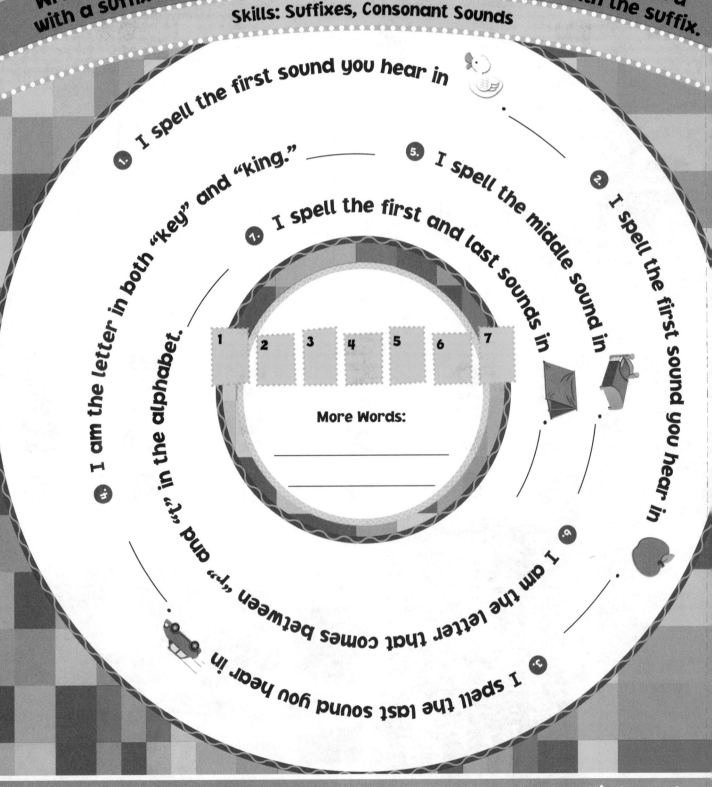

1. I spell the first sound you hear in 🐤 .

5. I spell the middle sound in 🎪 .

2. I spell the first sound you hear in 🍎 .

7. I spell the first and last sounds in 📬 .

6. I am the letter in both "key" and "king." ___

| 1 | 2 | 3 | 4 | 5 | 6 | 7 |

More Words:

_____

_____

4. I am the letter in the alphabet.

6. I am the letter that comes between "r" and "t" in the alphabet.

3. I spell the last sound you hear in 🚗 .

In Search Of

In each row, cross out the letter that you see the most. The rest of the letters will spell a preposition. On the lines, write each preposition you find.

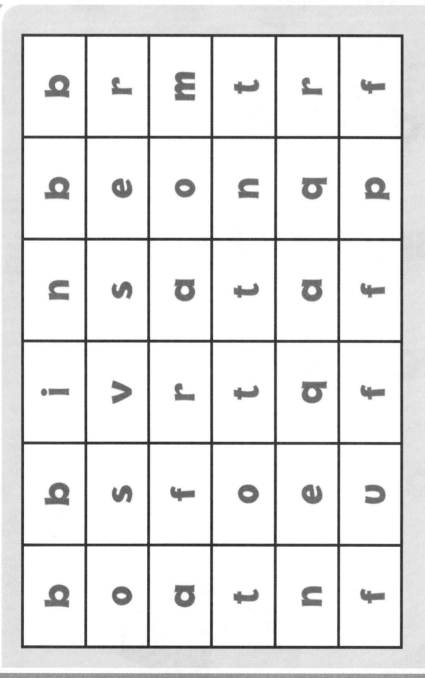

WORD MATH

Skills: Long and Short Vowel Sounds, Spelling

Write the word that solves each puzzle. In each word you write, circle the letters that spell the long or short vowel sound.

1. r + bed − b = _____

2. l + stamp − st = _____

3. s + bee − b = _____

4. b + rib − r = _____

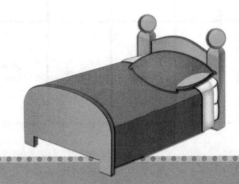

5. **wet** − **t** + **b** = _____

6. **r** + **cake** − **c** = _____

7. **s** + **top** = _____

8. **m** + **spoon** − **sp** = _____

Write each word under the fish that shows its beginning sound.

barn pen cut pig big cow bee cape pan

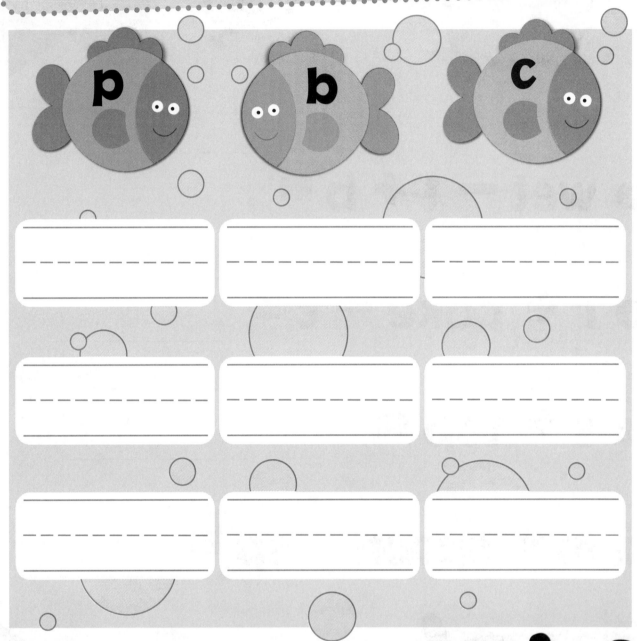

Picture This!

GO ON ACROSS

Name each picture.
Write the name in
the puzzle.

1.
2.
3.

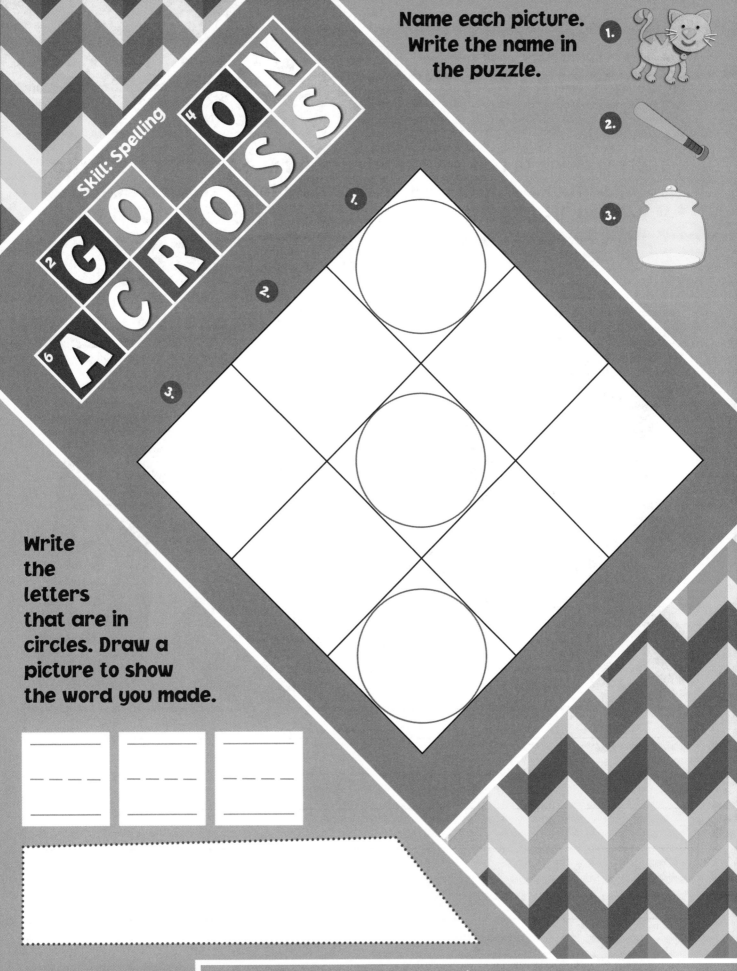

Write
the
letters
that are in
circles. Draw a
picture to show
the word you made.

Sentence Scramble

Draw a line to connect the words and make a sentence. Write the sentence on the lines. Add capital letters where they are needed. Use an end mark at the end of the sentence. Circle the word that has a prefix.

unhappy

tom

balloon

popped

was

when

the

JUMBLED UP

Cut out the tiles. Arrange them to make a sentence. Write the sentence on the lines. Use capital letters where they are needed. End your sentence with an end mark.

each day

my dad

the park

and I

go to

RIDDLE ME

Write the word that completes each hink pink.

Skills: Rhyming Words, Spelling

A hink pink is a pair of rhyming words that answer a riddle.

Example: long song

1. What is a boiling pan? a _____ pot

2. What is a chubby kitty? a _____ cat

3. What is a soggy dog? a _____ pet

4. What is a happy father? a _____ dad

5. What is a huge hog? a _____ pig

6. What is a cozy insect? a _____ bug

MIRROR
MIRROR

1 **2**

1. snowman

2. fin

3. bucket

4. slip

5. log

6. sheep

7. pancake

8. mud

Hold the page up to a mirror to read the words. Say each word, clapping once for each syllable you hear. Circle the clapping hands to show how many syllables each word has.

MAZE CRAZE

Skills: Question Words, Letter Recognition

Cross out all the uppercase letters. The letters that are left will spell five question words. Write the question words on the lines.

V	B	w	h	o	D	J
M	Q	s	B	h	o	W
G	W	h	a	t	H	R
I	X	y	w	h	e	n
P	E	w	h	y	y	K

_____

_____

_____

_____

_____

_____

_____

Use the code to write the letters in each word.

1.

_ _ _ _

2.

_ _ _

3.

_ _ _

4.

_ _ _ _

CODE BREAKER

Skills: Spelling, Sight Words

Code Key

a	b	e	h	m	n	t	u	w

Sudoku for you

Skill: Spelling

Write letters in the boxes so that each row and column has the letters to spell 🐦. Do not use any letter more than once in the same row or column.

b	o	_
_	y	b
_	_	_

1. ohrse

2. ishf

3.  oups

4.  albl

5.  ifgt

The first letter of each word is in the wrong place. Find the letter. Then, write the word that matches the picture.

Look at the words in each list. Their meanings are close but not the same. Cut out the words. Glue or tape each one in the correct list. Color each word to match its list.

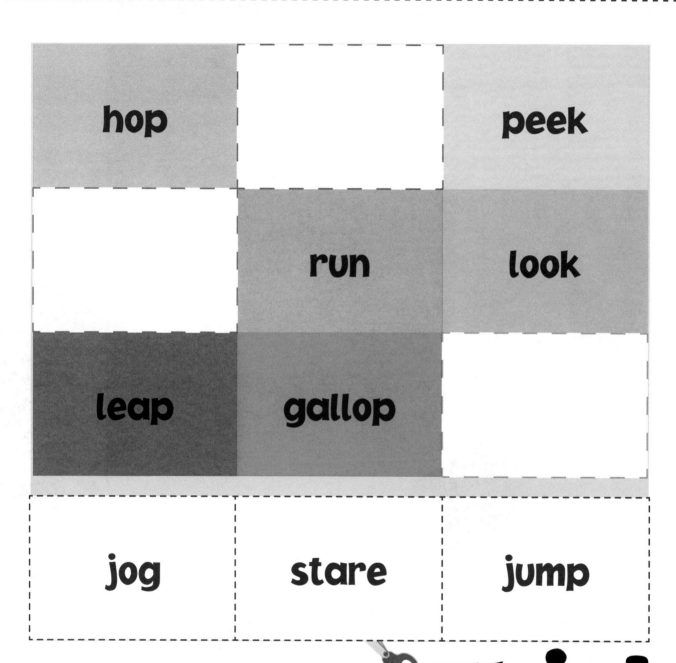

hop

peek

run

look

leap

gallop

jog

stare

jump

Picture This!

1. I am the opposite of "no." What word am I?

_____

2. I am something you do when you are hungry. What am I?

_____

3. Use me to be polite. What word am I?

_____

4. I am the opposite of "old." What word am I?

_____

5. I am "no" backward. What word am I?

_____

Use the clues to answer each question. Choose words from the word box.

Word Box

yes	eat
on	please
new	

Skill: Sight Words

QUIZ WHIZ

RIDDLE ME

Write a letter for each clue. Put the letters together to spell a word that can mean both "something to wear" and "look."

Skills: Vocabulary, Consonant Sounds

1. I spell the first sound you hear in

5. I spell the first sound you hear in

2. I spell the middle sound you hear in

4. I spell the first sound you hear in

3. I spell the last sound you hear in

1	2	3	4	5

1. Start with "T." Add a line at the bottom. What letter do you have?

_____

_ _ _ _ _ _ _

_____

2. What letter looks like "q" backward?

_____

_ _ _ _ _ _ _

_____

3. Take away the bottom bump of "B." What letter do you have?

_____

_ _ _ _ _ _ _

_____

4. Take away the top two lines of "E." What letter do you have?

_____

_ _ _ _ _ _ _

_____

5. What letter looks like half of "w"?

_____

_ _ _ _ _ _ _

_____

How well do you know your letters? It is time to find out! Write a letter to answer each question.

Letter Box

P	p
L	I
V	

QUIZ WHIZ

Skills: Letter Recognition, Handwriting

PREST-O

CHANGE-O!

Skill: Long and Short Vowel Sounds

Read each word with a long vowel sound. Cross out one letter. Write the new word that has a short vowel sound. Use the picture clues to help you.

vain

teen

hope

soon

main

mean

Skills: Nouns, Classifying

Fill in the chart. Write nouns that name people, places, and things and that begin with the letters shown. Some are done for you.

Nouns

Letter	People	Places	Things
a		airport	
h			
k	kids		
n			
s			sock
w			

ALPHA-CHALLENGE

Skill: Consonant Sounds

GO ACROSS

Say the name of each picture. In the puzzle, write the letter that makes its beginning sound. Then, read the word formed in each row. Color the picture that matches.

1.
2.
3.

4.
5.
6.

In Search Of

Find and circle these words:

- brown
- want
- they
- must
- all
- saw
- out
- did

The word search grid:

```
              F
              J U
          N N F D T
        W N A B H H A
      A O Y N D T D F
    A H R N A B S A D L
  C A B M G L A F L S
  T A R W Y H F O D E
J F C O N B S U
P T X W N H M T W
  K H E Q J X U Q
S L F C B A Y P S N Z
  O T Z R N M W K H X
    K E V O U Q J V W J F
      C W S S J Y D Y I S
        B N M T W T S X W
          R C L U Q W X F
            O I N S U N M
              W E T K H X
                N Z M P W
              Y C T D Y F
              P N U S I D
                C A D T Y
                E A D A I
                U T D L S
                J M A M X
                F Q L W
                T O M T
                D H Q H
                G E T E
                S W N Y
                N P M D
                W P Q
                D P T
                S D N
                A O M
                W K
                R B B W Y C
                  Q T C Q
                N O K
                  B
```

JUMBLED UP

Skills: Suffixes, Base Words

Match each base word with a suffix. Write the words on the lines.

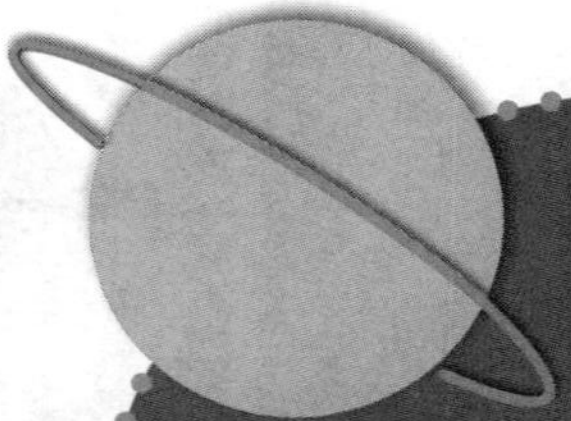

eat	end
kiss	farm
fast	joy

-est	-er
-ful	-es
-ing	-ed

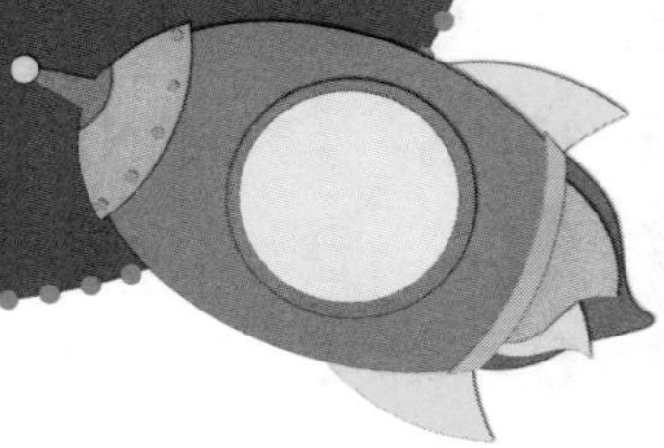

Skill: Long Vowel Sounds

IN PIECES

Cut out the pieces. Say the name of each picture. Match each picture with its long vowel sound.

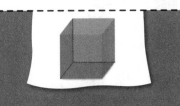

RIDDLE ME

Write a letter for each clue. Put the letters together to find the answer to the riddle.

Skills: Consonant Sounds, Spelling

1. This letter is in [donkey] but not in [boat]

2. This letter is in [glove] but not in [hat]

3. This letter is in [mop] but not in [panda]

4. This letter is in [bus] but not in [calendar]

5. This letter is in [pen] but not in [pin]

(center) I have a thumb and four fingers, but I am not alive. I am a . . .

Answer:

1	2	3	4	5

MIRROR
MIRROR

1.	win	lose	👍 👎
2.	out	in	👍 👎
3.	quick	fast	👍 👎
4.	hop	jump	👍 👎
5.	down	up	👍 👎
6.	hard	soft	👍 👎
7.	tiny	small	👍 👎
8.	cold	hot	👍 👎

Hold up the page to a mirror to read each pair of words. Are they opposites? If they are, circle 👍. If they are not, circle 👎.

Say the names of the pictures on the rays of each sun. What sound do you hear at the beginning of each one? Write the letter that makes that sound in the center of each sun.

Picture This!

WORD MATH

Write the word that solves each puzzle. If the word is a noun, circle "N." If the word is a verb, circle "V."

1. 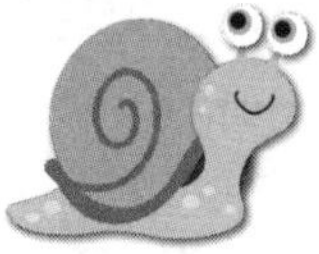 🐌 − s = _____   Ⓥ   Ⓝ

2. 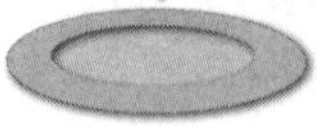 🍽 − te + y = _____   Ⓥ   Ⓝ

3. 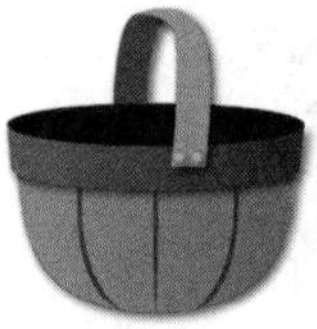 🧺 − b − et = _____   Ⓥ   Ⓝ

4. r + ☀ − s = _____   Ⓥ   Ⓝ

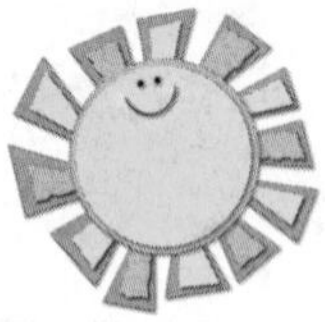

5. v +  − n =

Ⓥ   Ⓝ
_____
- - - - - - - - -
_____

6. b +  − r =

Ⓥ   Ⓝ
_____
- - - - - - - - -
_____

7. j +  − n =

Ⓥ   Ⓝ
_____
- - - - - - - - -
_____

8. w +  − p =

Ⓥ   Ⓝ
_____
- - - - - - - - -
_____

Cross out all the lowercase letters. The letters that are left will spell six words. Use lowercase letters to write them on the lines.

H	A	V	E	b	r	s
i	I	N	T	o	m	f
g	v	q	u	o	u	R
S	A	y	x	a	o	l
j	c	w	E	L	l	m
t	e	a	H	E	y	b

MAZE CRAZE

Sudoku for you

Skills: Spelling, Opposites

Write letters in the boxes so that each row and column has the letters to spell the opposite of "high." Do not use any letter more than once in the same row or column.

	M	
O	W	W
		1

Sentence Scramble

Draw a line to connect the words and make a sentence. Write the sentence on the lines. Add capital letters where they are needed. Use an end mark at the end of the sentence. Then, do what the sentence tells you to do!

the

three

march

times

around

room

MAZE CRAZE

Skills: Consonant Sounds, Writing Sentences

Help the turtle find the pond. Color each word that has the same beginning sound as to make a path. Then, use two words you colored to write a sentence on the lines.

tub	wet	pal	rest
ten	leg	let	fun
tip	I	last	can
tan	tent	today	tag
bun	pen	sit	tug

Skill: Spelling

GO ON ACROSS

²G O ⁴O N
A C R O S S

Name each picture. Write the name in the puzzle.

1.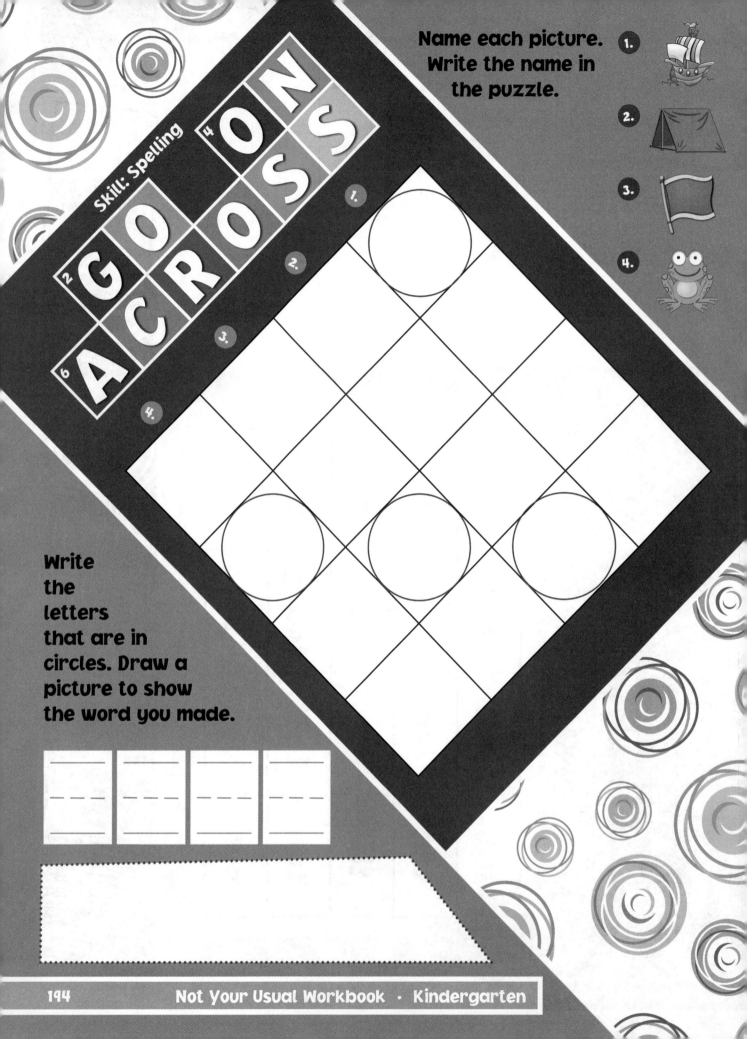
2.
3.
4.

Write the letters that are in circles. Draw a picture to show the word you made.

Skill: Parts of a Book

Cut out the words. Tape or glue them in the spaces to label the parts of a book.

Into the Jungle

Written by Li Chen

Pictures by Matt Hart

Title	Author	Illustrator	Front Cover

Picture This!

CODE BREAKER

Skills: Spelling, Long Vowel Sounds

Use the code to write each long vowel word.

1. sl   p

2. c  t

3.   t

4. b  k

5. tr  in

6. f   d

Code Key

a	e	i	o	u
		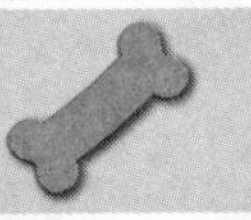		

Match the prefixes with the base words. Write the new words on the lines.

un–   dis–

re–   non–

stop   fair

like   do

tell   play

In Search Of

Read the words in each row. Color two that have the same ending sound. On the line, write the letter that makes the ending sound.

sack	nine	sat	map	let	bag
pat	ice	said	cot	fell	rug
pass	fun	sip	red	fast	race
kite	not	kite	cab	sail	best
kiss	fast	tape	crab	ship	game

Sentence Scramble

Draw a line to connect the words and make a sentence. Write the sentence on the lines. Add capital letters where they are needed. Use an end mark at the end of the sentence. Circle two words that are opposites.

MIRROR

1. leap — hop

2. walk — run

3. gulp — sip

4. awful — bad

5. pour — drizzle

6. night — day

7. huge — big

8. hot — warm

Hold up the page to a mirror to read each pair of words. Do they have similar meanings? If they do, write a check mark (✔) in the box.

Think about a favorite story. It could be a fairy tale like "Goldilocks and the Three Bears." It could be a favorite book you have at home. Follow the directions.

Draw people or animals from the story (characters).

Draw a place where the story takes place (setting).

Draw something that happens in the story (event).

Picture This!

Park next to the van.

We play ball at the park.

Dad got a new watch.

IN PIECES

Cut out the pieces. Match each sentence with a picture that shows the meaning of the word shown in white.

I like to watch birds.

My dogs bark a lot.

The tree's bark is brown.

PREST-O

Skills: Consonant Sounds, Rhyming Words

Write words to match the picture clues. Each word should be the same as the one above it except for one changed letter.

CHANGE-O!

Unscramble the letters to spell nouns. Then, draw a line to match each noun to a picture.

1. eetr _____

2. cta _____

3. pto _____

4. rdmu _____

5. ebno _____

ANSWER KEY

Page 8

Page 9

Page 10

Page 11

Not Your Usual Workbook · Kindergarten

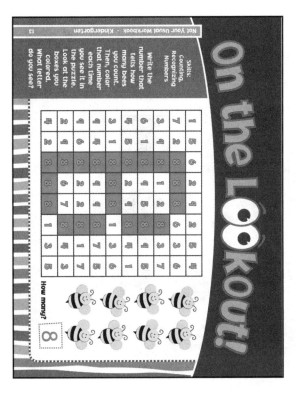

Page 13

Page 14

Page 15

Page 16

Page 17

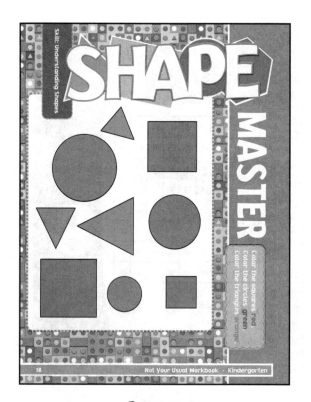

Page 18

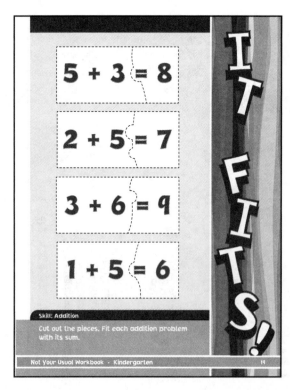

Page 19

Page 21

Page 22

Page 23

Page 24

Page 25

Page 26

Page 27

Page 28

Page 29

Not Your Usual Workbook · Kindergarten 31

On the Lookout!

Skill: Place Value

Read each description. Circle the correct number.

10 ones and 4 ones
10 ones and 7 ones
10 ones and 2 ones
10 ones and 5 ones
10 ones and 4 ones

16 14 17 10 12
17 15 18 11 13
18 16 19 12 14
19 17 20 13 15

Page 31

STORY STUMPERS

Solve each story problem. Use the pictures to help you find the answer.

Skill: Word Problems

1. There were 5 trees in the yard. We planted 3 more trees. How many trees are in the yard now?

8 trees

2. 4 frogs croaked. Then, 3 more frogs began to croak. How many frogs were croaking in all?

7 frogs

3. 6 cars were parked in a lot. Then, 2 more cars parked there. How many cars in all were parked in the lot?

8 cars

32 Not Your Usual Workbook · Kindergarten

Page 32

QUICK DRAW

Use the four small triangles to draw one big triangle. Use the four small squares to draw one big square.

Skill: Drawing Shapes

Not Your Usual Workbook · Kindergarten 33

Page 33

NUMBER CROSS

Skill: Addition Subtraction

Solve each problem. Write the answer in the puzzle.

1. 2 + 7 = _____
2. 2 + 6 = _____
3. 2 + 5 = _____
4. 2 + 4 = _____
5. 2 + 3 = _____
6. 9 − 5 = _____
7. 9 − 6 = _____
8. 9 − 7 = _____
9. 9 − 8 = _____

9 8 7
6 5 4
3 2 1

34 Not Your Usual Workbook · Kindergarten

Page 34

Page 35

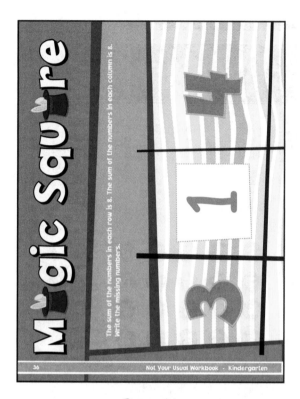

Page 36

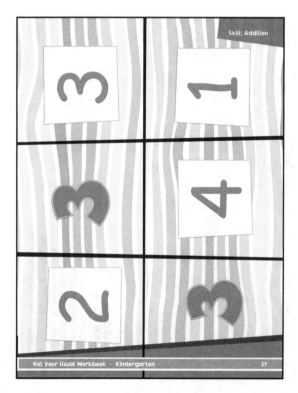

Page 37

Page 38

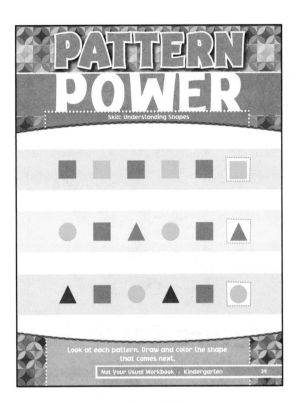

Page 39

Page 40

Page 41

Page 43

Page 44

Page 45

Page 46

Page 47

Page 49

Page 50

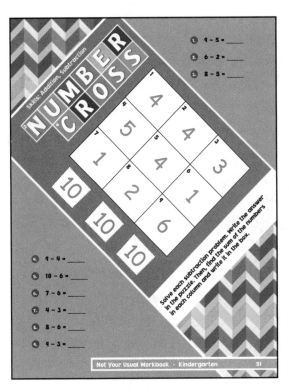

Page 51

Page 52

Page 53

Page 54

Page 55

Page 56

Page 57

Page 59

Page 60

Page 61

Page 62

Page 63

Page 64

Page 65

Page 67

Page 68

Page 69

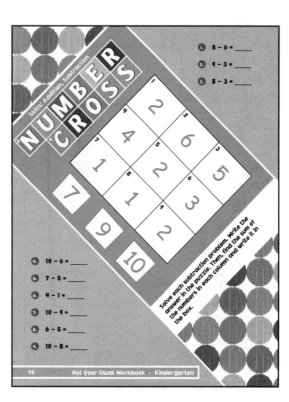

Page 70

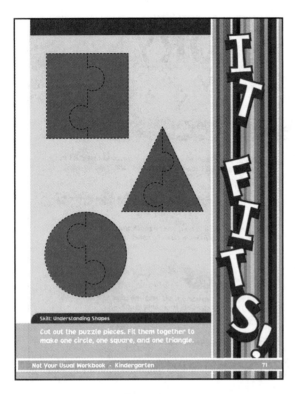

Page 71

Page 73

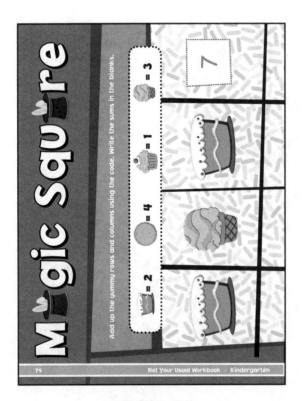

Page 74

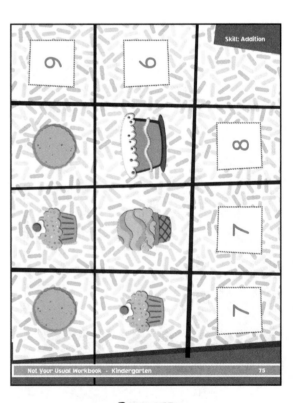

Page 75

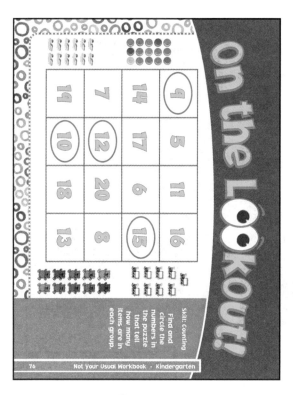

Page 76

Page 77

Page 78

Page 79

DARE TO DECODE

Skill: Place Value

Use the addition problems to crack the code. One number is given for you.

Code Key

●	◆	■	▲	○	⬡	★
4	2	5	1	10	8	9

● + ■ = 15   ○ + ◆ = 12

● + ● = 14   ○ + ⬡ = 18

● + ▲ = 11   ○ + ★ = 19

Not Your Usual Workbook · Kindergarten   80

Page 80

Skill: Comparing Weight

Cut out the items. Glue or tape them onto the scales to make each picture true.

A Show of Hands

Answers may vary. Possible answers shown.

Not Your Usual Workbook · Kindergarten   81

Page 81

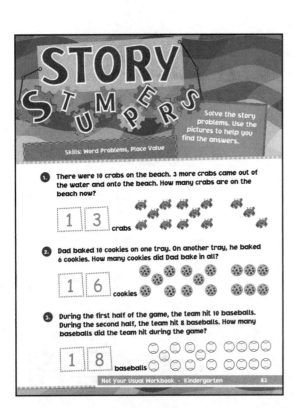

STORY STUMPERS

Skills: Word Problems, Place Value

Solve the story problems. Use the pictures to help you find the answers.

1. There were 10 crabs on the beach. 3 more crabs came out of the water and onto the beach. How many crabs are on the beach now?

   1 3 crabs

2. Dad baked 10 cookies on one tray. On another tray, he baked 6 cookies. How many cookies did Dad bake in all?

   1 6 cookies

3. During the first half of the game, the team hit 10 baseballs. During the second half, the team hit 8 baseballs. How many baseballs did the team hit during the game?

   1 8 baseballs

Not Your Usual Workbook · Kindergarten   83

Page 83

Shapes are all around you. Look around the room, out the window, or outside. Find an example of each shape. Draw what you see.

DRAW QUICK

Skill: Drawing Shapes

Drawings will vary.

Not Your Usual Workbook · Kindergarten   84

Page 84

Page 85

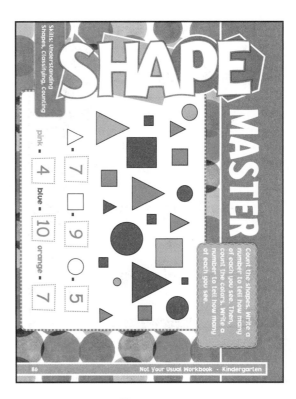

Page 86

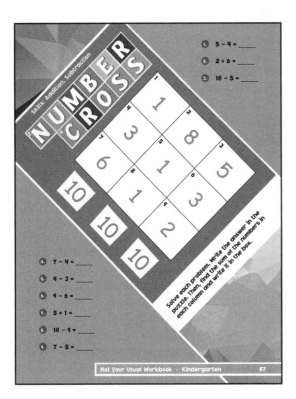

Page 87

Page 88

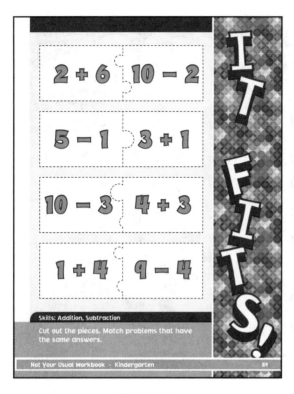

Page 89

Page 91

Page 92

Page 93

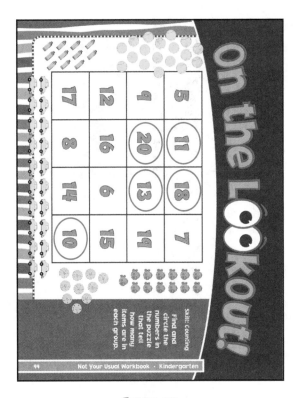

Page 94

Page 95

Page 96

Page 97

Page 98

Page 99

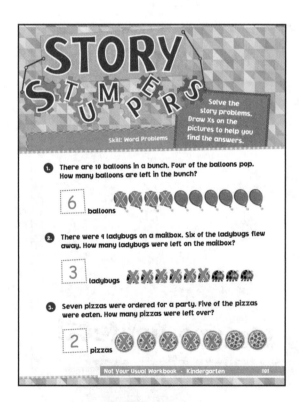

Page 101

Page 102

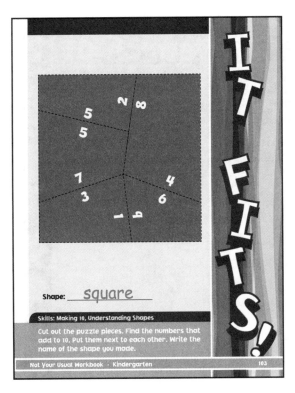

Page 103

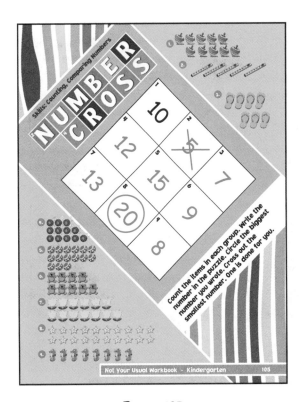

Page 105

Page 106

Page 108

Page 109

Page 110

Page 111

Page 113

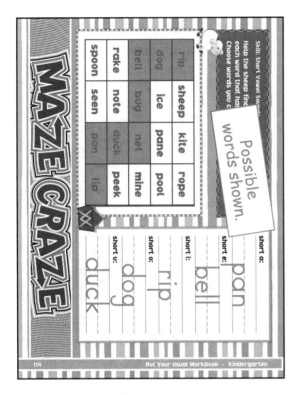

Page 114

Page 115

Page 116

Page 117

Page 119

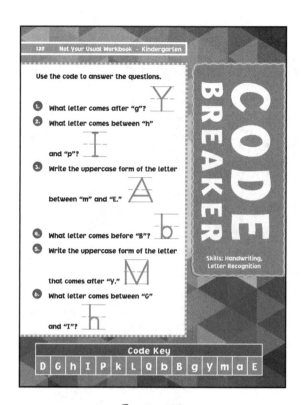

Page 120

Page 121

Page 122

Page 123

Page 124

Page 125

Page 126

Page 127

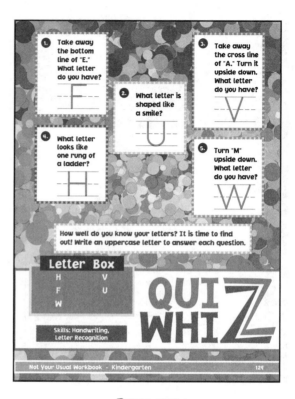

Page 129

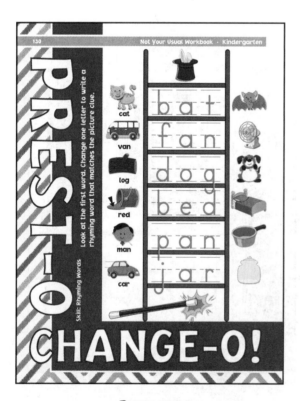

Page 130

Page 131

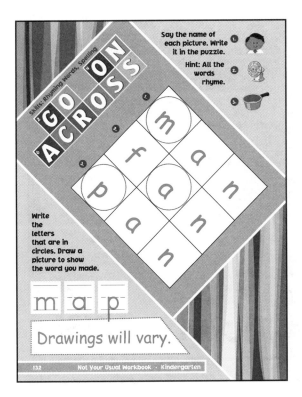

Page 132

Page 133

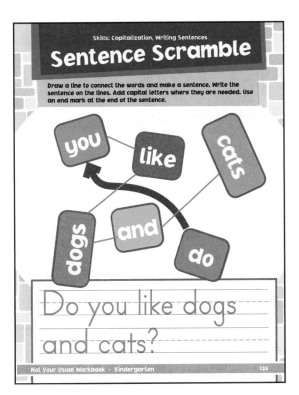

Page 135

Page 136

Page 137

Page 138

Page 139

Page 140

Page 141

Page 142

Page 143

Page 144

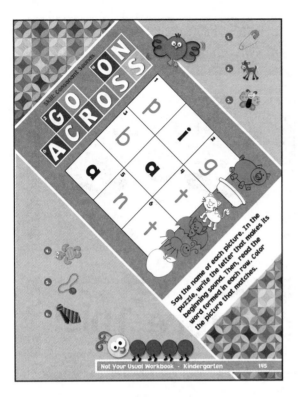

Page 145

Page 146

Page 147

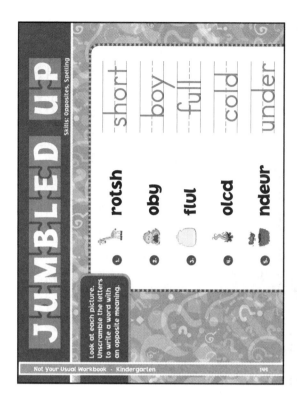

Page 149

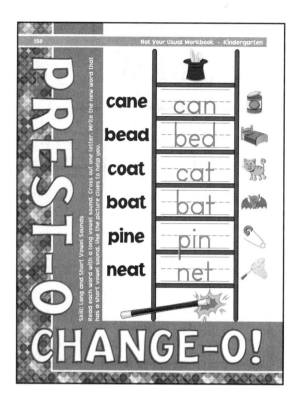

Page 150

Page 151

Page 152

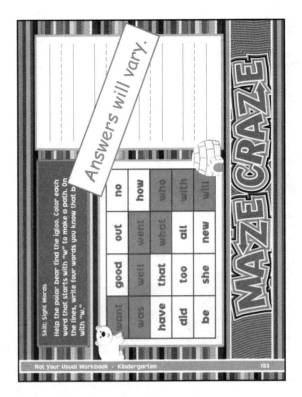

Page 153

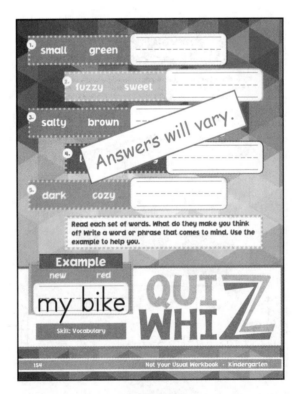

Page 154

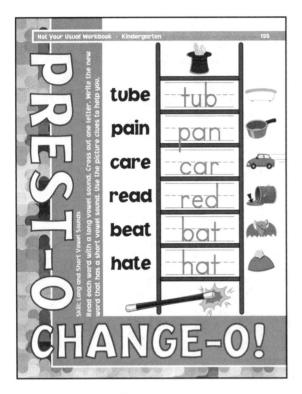

Page 155

Page 156

Page 157

Page 158

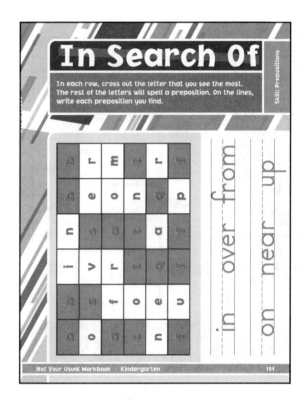

Page 159

Page 160

Page 161

Page 162

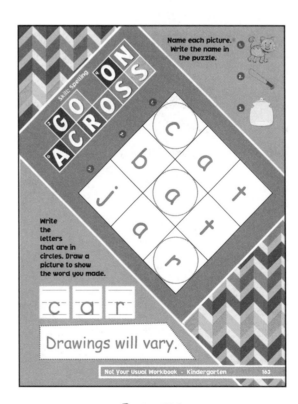

Page 163

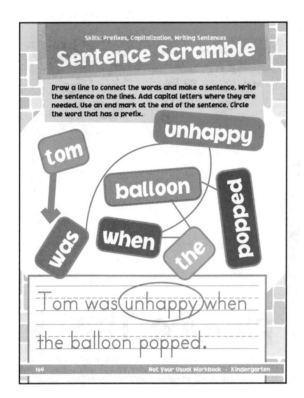

Page 164

Page 165

Page 167

Page 168

Page 169

Page 170

Page 171

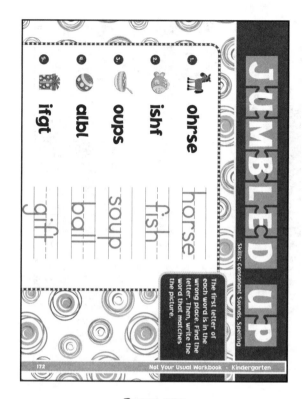

Page 172

Page 173

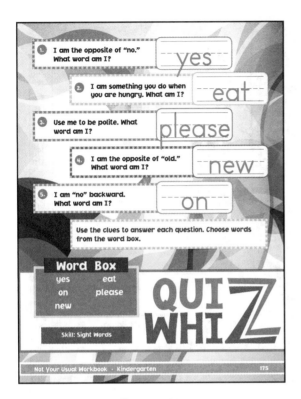

Page 175

Page 175 content

1. I am the opposite of "no." What word am I?
   yes

2. I am something you do when you are hungry. What am I?
   eat

3. Use me to be polite. What word am I?
   please

4. I am the opposite of "old." What word am I?
   new

5. I am "no" backward. What word am I?
   on

Use the clues to answer each question. Choose words from the word box.

Word Box
yes   eat
on   please
new

QUIZ WHIZ

Skill: Sight Words

Page 176 content

RIDDLE ME

rite a letter or each clue. ut the letters together to spell a word that can mean both somethin to ear and look.

Skills: Vocabulary, Consonant Sounds

- I spell the first sound you hear in (cake) . c
- I spell the first sound you hear in (worm) . w
- I spell the first sound you hear in (ball) .
- I spell the middle sound you hear in (frog) .
- I spell the last sound you hear in (witch) .

w a t c h
1 2 3 4 5

Page 176

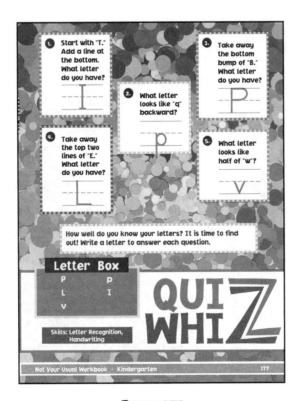

Page 177

Page 177 content

1. Start with "T." Add a line at the bottom. What letter do you have?
   I

2. What letter looks like "q" backward?
   p

3. Take away the bottom bump of "B." What letter do you have?
   P

4. Take away the top two lines of "E." What letter do you have?
   L

5. What letter looks like half of "w"?
   v

How well do you know your letters? It is time to find out! Write a letter to answer each question.

Letter Box
P   p
L   I
v

QUIZ WHIZ

Skills: Letter Recognition, Handwriting

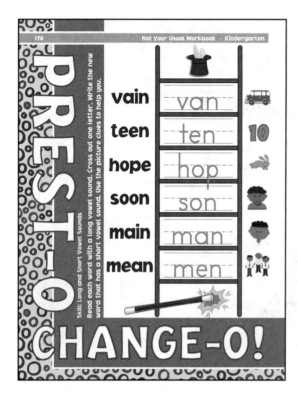

Page 178

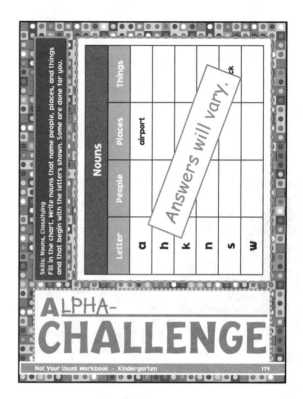

Page 179

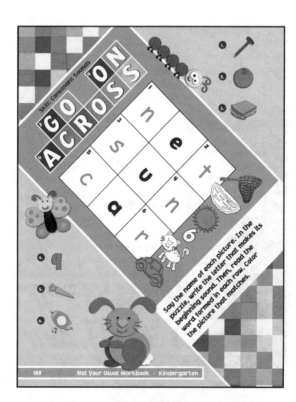

Page 180

Page 181

Page 182

Page 183

Page 185

MIRROR

MIRROR

Skill: opposites

1.	win	lose	👍 👎
2.	out	in	👍 👎
3.	quick	fast	👍 👎
4.	hop	jump	👍 👎
5.	down	up	👍 👎
6.	hard	soft	👍 👎
7.	tiny	small	👍 👎
8.	cold	hot	👍 👎

Hold up the page to a mirror to read each pair of words. Are they opposites? If they are, circle 👍. If they are not, circle 👎.

186

Not Your Usual Workbook · Kindergarten

Page 186

Skill: Consonant Sounds

Say the names of the pictures on the rays of each sun. What sound do you hear at the beginning of each one? Write the letter that makes that sound in the center of each sun.

Picture This!

Not Your Usual Workbook · Kindergarten   187

Page 187

Page 188

Page 189

Page 190

Page 191

Page 192

Page 193

Page 194

Page 195

Page 197

Page 198

Page 199

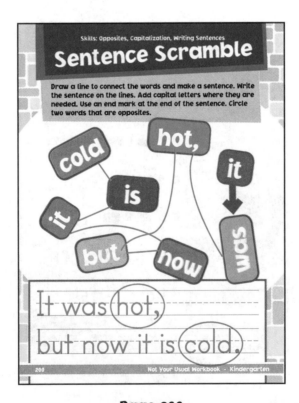

Page 200

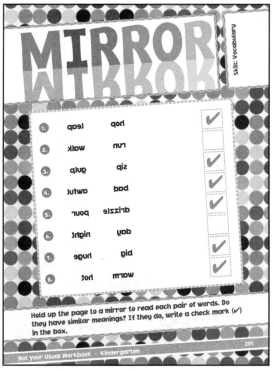

Page 201

Skill: Vocabulary

MIRROR
MIRROR

1. leap   hop   ✓
2. walk   run
3. gulp   sip
4. awful   bad   ✓
5. pour   drizzle
6. night   day
7. huge   big   ✓
8. warm   hot   ✓

Hold up the page to a mirror to read each pair of words. Do they have similar meanings? If they do, write a check mark (✓) in the box.

Not Your Usual Workbook · Kindergarten   201

Page 202

Skill: Characters, Settings, and Events

Think about a favorite story. It could be a fairy tale like "Goldilocks and the Three Bears." It could be a favorite book you have at home. Follow the directions.

Draw people or animals from the story (characters).

Draw a place where the story takes place (setting).

Drawings will vary.

Draw something that happens in the story (event).

Picture This!

202   Not Your Usual Workbook · Kindergarten

Page 203

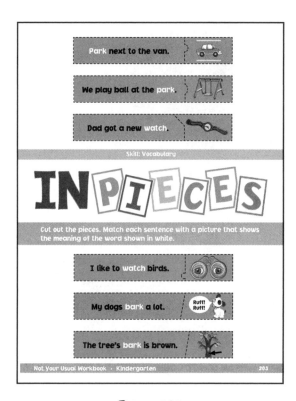

Park next to the van.

We play ball at the park.

Dad got a new watch.

Skill: Vocabulary

IN PIECES

Cut out the pieces. Match each sentence with a picture that shows the meaning of the word shown in white.

I like to watch birds.

My dogs bark a lot.   Ruff! Ruff!

The tree's bark is brown.

Not Your Usual Workbook · Kindergarten   203

Page 205

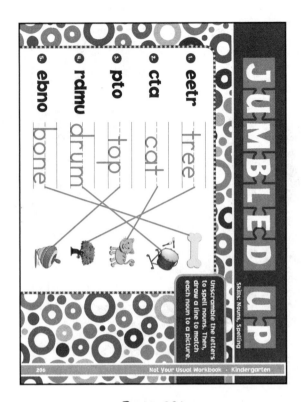

Page 206